The Great Depression and the New Deal:
A Very Short Introduction

VERY SHORT INTRODUCTIONS are for anyone wanting a stimulating and accessible way in to a new subject. They are written by experts, and have been published in more than 25 languages worldwide.

The series began in 1995, and now represents a wide variety of topics in history, philosophy, religion, science, and the humanities. Over the next few years it will grow to a library of around 200 volumes — a Very Short Introduction to everything from ancient Egypt and Indian philosophy to conceptual art and cosmology.

Very Short Introductions available now:

Available soon:

For more information visit our web site
www.oup.co.uk/general/vsi/

Eric Rauchway

THE GREAT DEPRESSION & THE NEW DEAL

A Very Short Introduction

OXFORD
UNIVERSITY PRESS

OXFORD
UNIVERSITY PRESS

Oxford University Press, Inc., publishes works that further
Oxford University's objective of excellence
in research, scholarship, and education.

Oxford   New York
Auckland   Cape Town   Dar es Salaam   Hong Kong   Karachi
Kuala Lumpur   Madrid   Melbourne   Mexico City   Nairobi
New Delhi   Shanghai   Taipei   Toronto

With offices in
Argentina   Austria   Brazil   Chile   Czech Republic   France   Greece
Guatemala   Hungary   Italy   Japan   Poland   Portugal   Singapore
South Korea   Switzerland   Thailand   Turkey   Ukraine   Vietnam

Copyright © 2008 by Oxford University Press, Inc.

Published by Oxford University Press, Inc.
198 Madison Avenue, New York, NY 10016

www.oup.com

Oxford is a registered trademark of Oxford University Press

Library of Congress Cataloging-in-Publication Data
Rauchway, Eric.
The Great Depression and the New Deal : a very short introduction /
Eric Rauchway.
p. cm.— (Very short introductions ; 166)
Includes bibliographical references and index.
ISBN 978-0-19-532634-5 (pbk.)
1. United States—History—1919-1933. 2. United States—History—1933-1945.
3. Depressions—1929—United States. 4. New Deal, 1933-1939.
5. United States—Economic conditions—1918-1945.
6. United States—Social conditions—1933-1945.
7. Roosevelt, Franklin D. (Franklin Delano), 1882-1945.
8. Depressions—1929—Europe.
9. Europe—Economic conditions—1918-1945. I. Title.
E806.R38 2008   973.91—dc22   2007030523

7 9 8 6

Printed in Great Britain by
Ashford Colour Press Ltd. Gosport, Hampshire

Contents

Acknowledgments

I owe most to scholars cited in the text and am additionally grateful to Alan Brinkley, Greg Clark, Andrew Cohen, Meg Jacobs, Ari Kelman, David Kennedy, Peter Lindert, Alan Olmstead, Kathy Olmsted, Steve Sheffrin, Alan M. Taylor, Louis Warren, undergraduates enrolled in History 174B at UC Davis in Spring 2007, and the conscientious referees and staff of the press for valuable comments and conversations about the Great Depression and New Deal.

List of Illustrations

Introduction

In 1932 the United States economy stood at its lowest ebb in modern history. An army of out-of-work military veterans camped and marched in Washington, DC. Unemployment stood at around 25 percent. Indeed the entire world seemed to have ground to a halt. Facing this crisis, Franklin D. Roosevelt accepted the Democratic nomination for president, pledging himself to "a new deal for the American people."[1] In that speech alone, elements of the "new deal" included increasing public works, supporting agricultural prices, creating new mortgage markets, shortening the working day and week, regulating securities, restoring international trade, reforesting the countryside, and repealing Prohibition. After taking office in 1933, Roosevelt worked with Congress to get laws passed for all these measures and more: by the end of the decade, the New Deal had grown to include social insurance against old age, unemployment, and disability; watershed management; support for unionization; deposit insurance; and a strengthened Federal Reserve System, among other innovations.

The New Deal included a variety of sometimes contradictory components that scholars still struggle to summarize. Often historians agree with Isaiah Berlin, who said in 1955 that the New Deal was an impressive balancing act, able "to reconcile individual liberty . . . with the indispensable minimum of organising and authority."[2] But as David M. Kennedy notes, we can see the New Deal thus only when it is "illumined by the stern-lantern of history."[3] Listening to Roosevelt's pledges in 1932, watching Congress pour reforms forth in the first one hundred days of his administration in 1933, seeing the White House reply to challenges from the Supreme Court and political opponents in 1935, hearing Roosevelt campaign as "the master" of corporate interests in 1936, it would have been hard to discern in advance what seemed clear in the wake of the decade's passing. And indeed, there is little proof that Roosevelt or anyone else set out to create the carefully balanced system that the New Deal became: it evolved as the president and Congress responded to the judiciary, the electorate, and the changing world of the Depression.

In this very short introduction to the Great Depression and the New Deal, I offer some basic ideas for a first understanding of this profound crisis and America's still-influential legislative response. The world that broke down in 1929 broke down for reasons that astute observers had predicted in advance. The subsequent and nearly total failure to repair the damage owed to clear errors of judgment and action, and the prolonged misery that millions of people suffered could therefore have been lessened. Roosevelt and the Democratic Congresses of the New Deal era achieved a marked historical success by correcting those errors. They also committed errors of their own, and I do not slight them here. But in the 1936 election, the American voters overwhelmingly asked their leaders to forge forward with their experiments, mistakes aside, rather than return to the old and, to their minds, wholly discredited ways. This spirit of pragmatic experimentation became the basis for a generation's faith in the new American way, not just in the United States but around the world.

Now, if you doubt the story is quite so simple, and if you insist that these simple statements require qualifications and nuance, I shall have to concede the point—beyond the confines of this brief book, I greatly respect the complexity of this era and the scholarship covering it. On the principle that you will go on from here if you wish fully to appreciate the period, the book concludes with recommendations for further reading. But the body of the book sticks to these simpler lines of argument on the grounds that they serve as a useful introduction to the subject.

The Great Depression began in the late 1920s, not necessarily with the Great Crash of 1929 but around that time, and afflicted a world tied together by specific kinds of debts, both within and between countries. Chapter 1 outlines that world and America's peculiar place in it, explaining how it differed from the world before World War I, and emphasizing the vulnerabilities of the system as outlined by contemporary critics: the web of debt binding that world together looked fragile to its keenest observers.

Chapter 2 discusses the reactions to the crisis, first of the Federal Reserve System, which serves the United States as a central bank, and second of President Herbert Hoover and the Republican majority in Congress. Contrary to Democratic accusations, the Republicans did not do nothing—but Hoover's own principles prevented him from doing nearly enough, and the crisis worsened appallingly under his leadership.

Chapter 3 shows that the greatness of the Great Depression owes to its widespread impact. It afflicted all sections of the American economy and much of the world. Perhaps most importantly, it encouraged middle-class American taxpayers and voters to identify themselves with the unfortunate many, rather the fortunate few.

The discussion here of the New Deal, like all such discussions, requires a selective principle to explain what belongs under that rubric and what does not. You will find two in this book. The first is chronological. While writers sometimes use the term "New Deal" to refer to the modern Democratic Party's agenda, or indeed the expansion of the American state under any administration for any purpose after the Roosevelt era (a concept that sometimes goes under the name, "the New Deal order"), I concern myself in this book chiefly with the 1930s—after which Roosevelt and his contemporaries thought the New Deal ended—and look only briefly to its legacy in the war years.[4] The second is functional. I divide the New Deal here into three parts: (1) those measures that appear to have worked to reverse the Depression; (2) those that did not; and (3) those that had little to do with fighting the current disaster but served to prevent or soften future ones.

Beyond Roosevelt's core conviction that "[n]ecessitous men are not free men," little held the New Deal together.[5] New Deal programs embodied no single approach to political management of the economy. They originated in no single book, speech, or person's thoughts. In some instances, Roosevelt himself had little to do with, or even opposed, ultimately important and successful legislation. The New Deal emerged over time from the fights between the president, the Congress, the Supreme Court, all of them influenced by the electoral returns that time after time supported this continuing conflict, in the interests of creating a stronger country.

Chapter 4, "Reflation and Relief," covers the New Deal stabilization and shoring-up of America's banks, currency, and credit, and the simultaneous effort to supply immediate relief to the Depression's suffering millions while still keeping American traditions and institutions intact. These efforts alone, pursued vigorously, might eventually have ended the Depression, but New Dealers had greater ambitions.

Chapter 5, "Managing Farm and Factory," explains New Deal attempts to re-create the managed economy of World War I for the peacetime crisis of the 1930s. These efforts generated controversy at the time and in retrospect appear considerably ill-advised. But they had roots deep in American politics, and their failures helped turn the New Deal into the balanced mechanism it became.

4

Chapter 6, "Countervailing Power," considers the ways New Dealers tried to redistribute influence in the American economy. They did not use state redistribution of wealth through tax policy and welfare payments; rather, they used law to encourage interest groups and individual actors to act independently of their employers.

By 1936, the use of countervailing power had become a distinctive hallmark of the New Deal. Never so efficient as direct state action, the strategy of countervailing power allowed Roosevelt to, in Berlin's words, "establish new rules of social justice ... without forcing his country into some doctrinaire strait-jacket, whether of socialism or State capitalism, or the kind of new social organisation which the Fascist regimes flaunted as the New Order."[6] By such methods the New Deal gave weaker groups in society the ability to negotiate better deals in a marketplace it left substantially intact.

The book's final chapter shows that the American electorate ratified Roosevelt in the landslide victory of 1936 and explains why the New Deal nevertheless ground to a halt within a few years after that. The Supreme Court played its part, and so did Franklin Roosevelt's overreaching ambition. But so too did the results of their first experiments change some New Dealers' minds. And finally, the impending war in Europe and America's response to it set aside the New Deal's fiscal caution and experimental care.

The New Deal did not end the Great Depression. As one American who lived through the 1930s told Studs Terkel, "industries needed to make guns for World War II made that happen."[7] Unemployment did not return to its 1929 level until 1943.[8] But while we can therefore say that the New Deal did not finish the job, we cannot say that it was not working. Throughout the 1930s, with the exception of the recession in 1937–38, the economy was improving—growing on average 8 percent a year from 1933–37 and 10 percent a year from 1938–41, while unemployment fell steadily as well.[9] This impressive rate of recovery reminds us how far the United States had to go to recover from the Hoover era. It also helps explain why the New Deal achieved such political success.

As a program to reform the American and global political economy, the New Deal met with more ambiguous fortune because it blurred into the war. The New Deal started and mainly stayed a purely American set of solutions to a problem of global importance, although the Anglo-American trade agreement of 1938 pointed toward an international method of reviving the world economy. And while the postwar order that Roosevelt in his last years helped secure for the world owed much to New Deal methods of pragmatic experimentation and shifting power away from states, because the war began before the lessons of the New Deal had made themselves quite clear, observers could not readily disentangle the two great events. The moral clarity of the 1940s obscured the hard choices, partial successes, and political bargains of the 1930s.

In the conclusion I discuss the New Deal's influence on the postwar world through the Bretton Woods system of international agreements for economic stability, which endured until the 1970s. Not until then did the United States begin to retreat from its New Deal at home and abroad. And even after several subsequent decades during which politicians have led a revival in America's pre-1929 beliefs, claiming repeatedly that government is a problem, not a solution, for modern economies, the New Deal's basic commitment to shared responsibility for economic security and its skepticism toward the complete reliability of bankers, brokers, and corporate executives has not quite died.

Throughout this book, the reader will find these interpretations guided not only by the easier wisdom of scholarly hindsight, but also by the perceptive assessments of contemporary observers. Just as Americans enjoyed the great good fortune of Franklin Roosevelt's unique presidential competence in both peace and war, they had also among them a remarkable generation of social scientists and other political analysts. The book relies on them as much as on those who have followed them and profited from their vision. And on the advice of one of the most acute among them, we begin with a description of the world that came limping to a halt in the Great War of 1914–18.

Notes

1. "Text of Governor Roosevelt's Speech at the Convention Accepting the Nomination," *New York Times*, January 3, 1932, 8.
2. Isaiah Berlin, "President Franklin Delano Roosevelt," in *The Proper Study of Mankind: An Anthology of Essays*, ed. Henry Hardy and Roger Hausheer (London: Chatto and Windus, 1997), 636–37.
3. David M. Kennedy, *Freedom from Fear: The American People in Depression and War, 1929–1945* (New York: Oxford University Press, 1999), 365.
4. Steve Fraser and Gary Gerstle, eds., *The Rise and Fall of the New Deal Order, 1930–1980* (Princeton: Princeton University Press, 1989). On the New Deal's contribution to the later growth of the executive branch, see Theodore Lowi, *The End of Liberalism: The Second Republic of the United States* (New York: W. W. Norton, 1979).
5. Cited in Kennedy, *Freedom from Fear*, 280. See also Berlin, "President Franklin Delano Roosevelt."
6. Berlin, "President Franklin Delano Roosevelt," 629–30.
7. Studs Terkel, *Hard Times: An Oral History of the Great Depression* (New York: The New Press, 2000), 57.
8. Susan B. Carter et al., eds., *Historical Statistics of the United States, Earliest Times to the Present, Millennial Edition* (New York: Cambridge University Press, 2006), series Ba475. Unemployment as a percentage of the civilian labor force was 2.9 percent in 1929; 3.1 percent in 1942 and 1.8 percent in 1943.
9. Christina D. Romer, "What Ended the Great Depression?," *Journal of Economic History* 52, no. 4 (1992): 757.

Chapter 1
The World in Debt

However various the explanations for the Great Depression have grown, they share an understanding that the world wracked by the crisis of the late 1920s differed significantly from the world in which most people had grown up. Inasmuch as the world had a single, integrated economy, it had recently undergone profound changes as a result of World War I. The war made it harder for people, goods, and money to move around the globe, and it shifted the direction in which they flowed, too. Putting the United States at the center of this new system, the war also changed America, rendering the once-peripheral New World nation's peculiarities central to the planet's concerns. Nor do these events and their potential for disaster appear only in retrospective clarity—some observers saw them coming.

Looking forward from the Treaty of Versailles at 1919, the economist John Maynard Keynes forecast what lay in wait for the industrial world: "depression of the standard of life of the European populations to a point which will mean actual starvation for some (a point already reached in Russia and approximately reached in Austria). Men . . . in their distress may overturn the remnants of organisation, and submerge civilisation itself in their attempts to satisfy desperately the overwhelming needs of the individual."[1] Depression, desperation, and the dismantling of civilization would result, Keynes wrote, from "the economic consequences of the peace," and although Keynes, perhaps mistakenly, attributed this impending disaster partly to the treaty's provisions, he also criticized its omissions.[2] World leaders at Versailles might have restored and codified the global system that prevailed from about 1870 to 1914, a system Keynes described as an "economic Utopia." But they missed this chance, producing instead a world quite unlike Utopia.[3]

Before 1914, people, goods, and capital crossed national borders with relative impunity. In consequence, they had the greatest possible scope to seek a place where their work would yield the greatest possible profit. To a considerable extent, this movement across borders meant the export of excess from industrial Europe.

Between the middle of the nineteenth century and World War I, about fifty-five million people left Europe to find their fortune in New World nations. Mostly industrial workers looking for higher wages in a worldwide market for their labor, their departure from Europe decreased the supply of workers there, raising wages for the laborers they left behind. Their arrival in the land-rich nations of the New World helped push development out into the frontiers. This migration did not occur altogether without hindrance. To describe the international markets of the nineteenth century as truly global represents some exaggeration, in large measure because New World nations preferred some parts of the globe over others when forging a cross-border market in, for example, labor. Notably, in the 1850s Australian states began limiting Chinese immigration, and by the early twentieth century the United States, Canada, and Australia all had erected high hurdles to immigration from both China and Japan; the United States in 1917 not only added a "barred zone" that blocked almost all the rest of Asia but also adopted a literacy test to reduce the number of incoming people. Nevertheless, these restrictions let millions of immigrants, particularly from southern and eastern Europe, move to better employment in the New World.

During the same period, the British empire generally backed the free movement of goods across borders. The relatively untaxed passage of things in trade—raw materials and finished products alike—between the Old World and the New allowed each nation to produce mainly what it was best suited to make. Although countries of the era sometimes raised barriers to trade as they did to migration—Latin American countries had especially high tariffs—international trade moved with relative freedom, especially compared to the 1920s, and Britain led in the promotion of lower tariffs.[4]

Observers noted that trade with Britain proved especially useful to many developing countries. British banks backed the builders of roads, canals, and railways as these countries stretched into their hinterlands and prairies. Bringing the fields under tillage made the New World more productive, and selling products back to their lender, Britain, helped developing countries defray their debts. Combined with the movement of goods and people, the movement of capital created a virtuous circle, at least so far as Europe was concerned. As a British economist wrote in 1909, "by the investment of capital in other lands we have, first, provided the borrowing countries with the credit which gave them the power to purchase the goods needed for their development, and secondly, enabled them to increase their own productions so largely that they have been able to pay us the interest and profits upon our capital and also to purchase greatly increased quantities of British goods."[5]

Keynes regarded this vanished system so highly because it had allowed Europe for the first time to relieve the pressure that an increase of population had appeared inexorably to put on the supply of food. Keynes explained: "With the growth of the European population there were more emigrants on the one hand to till the soil of the new countries, and, on the other, more workmen were available in Europe to prepare the industrial products and capital goods which were to maintain the emigrant populations in their new homes, and to build the railways and ships which were to make accessible to Europe food and raw products from distant sources."[6] The war shut down this system. People and goods could no longer move freely, and their formerly productive power went instead toward destruction. Capital funded the war's western front instead of the New World frontier. But worse, once the war ended, the peace did nothing to restore the lost world. "The Treaty includes no provisions for the economic rehabilitation of Europe ... or to adjust the systems of the Old World and the New," Keynes complained.[7]

Looking back from the 1930s, the British historian E. H. Carr wrote, "In 1918 world leadership was offered, by almost unanimous consent, to the United States ... it was then declined."[8] Most notably, the United States declined to lead the world in reconstructing the old, open economy. Indeed, it moved in the opposite direction.

The United States had tried to limit immigration before the war, but it turned to the task with greater energy and effectiveness in the 1920s. Congress established quota limits on immigration with the laws of 1921 and 1924. Other New World countries blocked immigration in their own ways. Some joined the United States in barring political radicals and classes of the criminal, poor, or disabled. Brazilians tried to steer immigration to farms, rather than cities. Canada's 1919 immigration act allowed officials to bar "immigrants ... deemed unsuitable owing to their peculiar customs, habits, [and] modes of life."[9] These restrictions made it harder for Europeans to find opportunities overseas, as Keynes had foreseen in 1919.

The movement in goods slowed owing to restrictive law as well. The United States raised tariffs in 1921 and 1922, and other countries began following suit. Alarmed diplomats convened conferences whose delegates advocated lifting these barriers, culminating with the League of Nations' World Economic Conference in 1927, which declared itself strongly against tariffs, to no effect. The Americans had a history of high tariffs stretching through the nineteenth century, but as the *New York Times* noted in 1926, circumstances had changed since then: "It needs no political economist to see that our situation in the world of trade has been radically altered by the events following 1914. A fiscal policy which might have been defensible before that year has since gone hopelessly awry. Our immense and increasing investments abroad cannot indefinitely be paid for unless we are willing to take what our foreign debtors can offer us."[10]

With the war the United States had switched positions, almost overnight, from the world's great debtor to the world's great creditor. New York replaced London as the central lender in the world's credit network. This move meant more than merely a shift in position and priority. Postwar debts differed from prewar borrowing. New World borrowers spent nineteenth-century British loans on railroads and ranches, building the capacity to repay their lenders. Belligerent borrowers spent wartime American loans on shot and shell, destroying that capacity. Nations wounded in war borrowed more money to repay their debts, sometimes borrowing from America to pay other belligerents who in turn paid America.

This new global system of the 1920s, less open and flexible than its predecessor, relied on continued American lending to fund deficits and debts around the war-impoverished world. And for a time, American lending served this purpose. Then, in 1928, it all but stopped, sending Germany, Poland, Brazil, Argentina, Australia, and Canada into recession.[11] But Americans were not looking at the limping world. They had their eyes on the racing economy at home.

After the United States recovered from a postwar recession in 1921, its economy grew at a healthy annual rate. American workers produced more goods more efficiently, and their incomes increased, if not quite so quickly as the profits born from their greater productivity.[12] Many Americans' optimism grew, too: they thought they had entered a new era of prosperity, when more Americans could afford more luxury goods and live, at least materially, better lives than ever before. So securely did they hold this belief that they accepted newly available offers of credit in order to buy what they could not afford from their own pockets. By the end of the decade Americans were living lives well-furnished with debt.

Before World War I, the average American household went a little more into debt each year—maybe a $4 increase over the year before, excluding mortgages. In the 1920s, the average increase more than tripled to about $14 a year.[13] With that borrowed money Americans bought the same goods they were increasingly making: expensive, durable, luxury items that gave them more varied amusements and higher expectations from life. The 1920s brought regular radio programs, and Americans bought radio sets and phonographs. They bought household appliances, like electric refrigerators. Most visibly, they bought cars.[14]

The production, purchase, and financing of automobiles drove the perception and reality of American prosperity in the 1920s. The output of America's automobile factories more than doubled over the decade, so that by 1929 the 4.4 million cars they produced were the single most valuable chunk of U.S. manufacturing output. At decade's end about 447,000 people worked in the automotive industry—only slightly fewer than worked in iron and steel, the nation's biggest manufacturing industry. The more cars Americans made, the more they drove up demand for glass, rubber, steel, and petroleum. Car-buyers drove the growth of roads, suburban houses, shopping centers, and other roadside attractions.[15]

In 1920 American motor vehicle bureaus recorded only one car registered for every three households; by the end of the decade the country had a car for almost every household. In 1929 there were about 23 million cars for a nation of about 123 million people: at a cozy fit of six per car, the whole country could have gone on the road at once.[16]

Henry Ford's motor company provided some of the technical and business innovations that made these changes possible. By World War I, Ford had settled on the Model T as its all-purpose consumer model, developed the moving assembly line as a method of mass production, and began touting the high wages its workers earned, as a way of ensuring their loyalty and their ability to purchase the company's signature product, whose price fell and fell over the years, from around $950 in 1909 to a low of $290 in 1926.[17]

Were Ford's the whole story of the automobile industry and, by extension, American manufacturing in the 1920s, it would sound something like this: higher wages, lower prices, and the mass production of a standard item made what was once a luxury into a commonly available commodity. But this is not the whole story. Despite the Model T's falling sticker price, major durable goods generally cost more in relation to other products in the 1920s than they had before the war. Americans did not buy these products in such quantities because they were cheap: they bought despite the expense.[18]

Ford's inexpensive, standard Model T made it possible for more, different people to own cars. But at some point, everyone who could afford a car would have one, and then who would buy? General Motors (GM) decided to make sure that the same people would keep buying different cars: it introduced planned obsolescence by annually changing its models, and to allow for the extravagance of regular new cars, GM began extending credit through the General Motors Acceptance Corporation.[19]

Often the ready credit of the 1920s came dear, at an annual interest rate of around 30 percent on an installment plan for a new car.[20] Even though moralists—Henry Ford among them—fretted over the ever-expanding definition of what Americans needed to buy, consumers themselves hearkened to the doctrine *Advertising and Selling* promulgated in 1926: "every free-born American has a right to name his own necessities."[21] Through the decade the list of these new necessities grew.

Yet credit could not stretch cash infinitely. Installment plans sent bills with clockwork regularity. Americans' income did not arrive with equal reliability: cyclical unemployment always loomed, and social insurance against it scarcely existed. So buyers had to take considerable care before they plunged into long-running debt. Any added uncertainty in consumers' outlook might make them wait, just a while, to see what might happen to affect their paychecks. In a time of economic crisis, even a short pause in purchasing could slow or even stop the nation's assembly lines.

As Americans eagerly heeded the advertisers' blandishments, they ran closer to the limits on their good fortune. The countries borrowing from the United States found out beginning in 1928 what happened when American credit dried up, and soon after Americans found out what happened when their own credit-fueled spending slowed. Both looked for the source of their problems and for possible solutions at the headwaters of debt in Wall Street.

If the world economy of the 1920s consisted of concentric circles, the outside ring held peoples remote from the industrial center and little touched by its booms and busts. The next ring inward included the industrial nations tied by debts to the United States. Next from them dwelt most of the Americans themselves, divided further into finer rings: those still struggling to get by, then those better off if perhaps in hock to fund their routine purchases, and then the minority—maybe under 10 percent—of Americans who owned stocks.[22] And inward at last from them lived the near-aristocracy, the moneymen who made decisions that determined how easily everyone else could get their credit and who increasingly fidgeted as they watched the stock-tickers.

The best-connected and most diligent public servants of their day worked on Wall Street and around it in lower Manhattan. In the 1920s they included the once and future Supreme Court Justice Charles Evans Hughes; the once and future Secretary of War Henry Stimson; the future New York governor Herbert Lehman; and the future president and sometime foe of all that Wall Street stood for, Franklin Roosevelt.[23] They handled mergers, stock offerings, and all the great business of the nation's businesses.

They also, along with their less reputable neighbors, handled other transactions. For example, with a sufficient sum of capital a group of investors could establish a "pool" specifically for the purpose of manipulating a stock. Members of the pool would buy and sell to one another at times and in increments calculated to tell a particular story to an outsider watching the ticker tape. The numbers on the tape showing the bare facts of trading did not lie, but the pattern of numbers might deceive an imaginative observer eager to know what the insiders knew. The ebb and flow of sales conducted among the members of a pool would intimate to an obsessed investor that someone, somewhere, had inside information that a company's stock should rise. Investors would flock to the pool stock, driving its price up. Then, when it seemed they had driven it as far as it would go, the original members of the pool would cash in, sending the price back down to its former level. It happened all the time and was not illegal. Nor was it even secret: the *Wall Street Journal* reported on the doings of pool stocks, published information about who led which pools, and trafficked regularly in the opinions of analysts as to which stocks best attracted uninformed enthusiasm ("anything which has electricity or light or power in its title," one analyst reported).[24]

Americans sometimes distinguished between this sort of activity, which they called "speculation," and ordinary purchase of stock, which they called "investing." Investors bought stock based on the soundness of the underlying enterprise over the long term, choosing securities on the basis of whether they thought the company would do its business competently in the months and years to come. Speculators bought and sold stock based on their intuitions as to everyone else's impulses in the market that day. And as speculative activity overshadowed investment, more speculators came into the market, and more observers worried.

By 1928, Wall Street men knew, and the *Wall Street Journal* affirmed, that they were working in "the kind of market that makes for larger commissions than profits."[25] Even so, increasing numbers of Americans wanted to play this evidently rigged game. People flocked to the big money, hoping to buy into the inner circle. Even a loss could give them the thrill of having brushed up against the big men.

Watching the increase in trading on the exchanges and in the borrowing to trade on the exchanges, the Federal Reserve decided to make it more expensive to borrow money. In June of 1928 the *Federal Reserve Bulletin* noted "an unprecedented volume of transactions on the exchange and a continued rise in security prices" while "brokers' loans reached a record figure...and continued to increase." So the Federal Reserve began "withdrawing funds from the money market."[26]

Yet speculation flourished into the new year. Early in 1929, just before Herbert Hoover's inauguration as president, the Federal Reserve warned publicly that it did not wish banks to use its credit for "maintaining speculative security loans."[27] Although speculation continued at a high rate, U.S. overseas investment did not: capital leaving America averaged around $800 million annually from 1925 to 1928, rising to $1,250 million in 1928, but fell to $628 million in 1929 and averaged about $360 million annually from 1929 to 1932.[28] The Federal Reserve's tighter monetary policy helped slow American capital going to foreign countries. Nations like Germany, which had depended on American loans, began to struggle under this handicap.

In later years, pronouncements reflecting incautious optimism, an insistence that everyone should become rich, that everything was for the best—comments so comforting to contemporaries and so reckless in retrospect—became a staple of every story about the Great Crash. And such remarks showed up all over in the weeks before they altogether ceased. Newspapers regularly sought the cheery views of professional soothers, who obligingly declared that they saw smooth sailing ahead. But by the late 1920s, a growing number of bankers and policymakers had the impression that the world simply could not sustain the current state of its finances. Both around the globe and within the United States too many people had borrowed too much money for unproductive purposes. The financier Bernard Baruch wrote, "Whereas it is wise to buy things on the partial payment plan that will result in time in increased economies and better living, at the same time it can be overdone. I am afraid it has now been overdone."[29]

Too few reliable investments remained. And even though only a few Americans actually bought and sold stocks, the market had become a kind of entertainment, a set-piece of idle chat. In itself, this prevalence of market talk warned those in the know that it was time to get out before it was too late. The financier Joseph P. Kennedy, who by summer of 1929 had sold out of his major holdings and kept his money in cash, advised a friend that "Only a fool holds out for the top dollar."[30] Self-aware fools went into the market assuming that still greater fools had yet to buy in. It took a shrewd judge of national character to decide just when the United States would run through its supply of fools.

Generally, those with means to leave Manhattan in summer regarded as fools those who stayed. Yet in August of 1929, traditionally a time to flee the city's unreasonable heat, the moneymen stayed in town to see if they could beat the big bull market as it rose. Even through Labor Day, even through hot days of high humidity, to the September 3 peak of market prices, they stayed. Then a few days later the market dropped a bit. A couple of weeks later it dropped a bit more.[31] The heat broke too. Rumors spread that the pool operators had decided to see if they could work their wiles in reverse and drive prices down. In the next weeks the market slid, rallied, and slid again.

Through the morning of October 24, in the streets of New York, crowds walked quietly downtown to Wall Street where they gathered silently and stood looking at the New York Stock Exchange, as if suddenly its abstract activities could become manifest, giving evidence of the disaster now plainly happening to them all.[32] That was Black Thursday. The market rallied afterward but then fell again. The oil tycoon John D. Rockefeller announced that "there is nothing in the business situation to warrant the destruction of values that has taken place" and that he was busy buying.[33] Neither this gesture nor others like it shored up stock prices. By mid-November, more than a third of the stock market's value had vanished.[34]

This fall in value immediately afflicted only a few Americans. But so closely had the others watched the market and regarded it as an index of their fates that they suddenly stopped much of their economic activity. As the economist Joseph Schumpeter later wrote, "people felt that the ground under their feet was giving way."[35] Facing a dubious future, Americans made important decisions not to buy. Particularly, they stopped buying the expensive durable goods like cars that they had learned to buy on credit. Each signature on an installment-plan contract represented a consumer's prediction about his or her ability to pay in the future. Suddenly Americans no longer felt able to see far enough ahead to make sound forecasts. Within a few months of the crash new car registrations had fallen by almost a quarter of their September number.[36] In 1930 spending on consumer durables fell by 20 percent.[37] Factories closed and banks failed. Unemployment more than doubled its 1929 level.

In 1931 John Maynard Keynes visited the United States and in a lecture attributed the increasingly severe Depression to "extraordinary imbecility."[38] On this point observers generally do agree: someone had blundered and, given the structure of global finance after World War I, that someone must have had an address ending in "United States of America." The principal candidate, then and later, was Herbert Hoover, who in his memoirs defended himself by agreeing with the earlier Keynes: "the primary cause of the Great Depression" Hoover wrote, "was the war of 1914–1918."[39] But Hoover stood little chance of escaping blame. By 1930 Joseph Kennedy was already calling one of Hoover's backers to say, "jot down the name of the next president.... It's Franklin D. Roosevelt."[40]

Notes

1. John Maynard Keynes, *The Economic Consequences of the Peace* (London: 1919), 213.
2. On Keynes's critique of reparations, see Niall Ferguson, *The Pity of War: Explaining World War I* (New York: Basic Books, 1999), 395–432.
3. Keynes, *Economic Consequences*, 8.
4. Christopher Blattman, Michael A. Clemens, and Jeffrey G. Williamson, "Who Protected and Why? Tariffs the World Around, 1870–1938," in *Conference on the Political Economy of Globalization* (2002), 30.
5. Eric Rauchway, *Blessed among Nations: How the World Made America* (New York: Hill and Wang, 2006), 156.
6. Keynes, *Economic Consequences*, 7.
7. Ibid., 211.
8. Edward Hallett Carr, *The Twenty Years' Crisis, 1919-1939*, 2nd ed. (London: Macmillan, 1962), 234.
9. Immigration Act, chap. 25 of 9–10 George V, p. 7, sec. 13, consulted online 2/27/2007, www.canadiana.org/ECO/ItemRecord/ 9_08048.
10. Rauchway, *Blessed among Nations*, 157.
11. Barry Eichengreen, "The Origins and Nature of the Great Slump Revisited," *Economic History Review* 45, no. 2 (1992): 223.
12. George Soule, *Prosperity Decade: From War to Depression, 1917-1929* (New York: Rinehart, 1947), 220.

13. Martha L. Olney, *Buy Now, Pay Later: Advertising, Credit, and Consumer Durables in the 1920s* (Chapel Hill: University of North Carolina Press, 1991), 91.

14. Ibid., 40.

15. Peter Fearon, *War, Prosperity, and Depression: The U.S. Economy, 1917–1945* (Oxford: Philip Allan, 1987), 55–56.

16. Soule, *Prosperity Decade*, 164.

17. John Bell Rae, *American Automobile Manufacturers* (Philadelphia: Chilton Company, 1959), 107–9; John Bell Rae, *The American Automobile* (Chicago: The University of Chicago Press, 1965), 61, 88.

18. Olney, *Buy Now*, 182.

19. Roland Marchand, *Advertising the American Dream: Making Way for Modernity, 1920–1940* (Berkeley: University of California Press, 1985), 156; Olney, *Buy Now*, 127.

20. Olney, *Buy Now*, 115.

21. Marchand, *Advertising the American Dream*, 160.

22. Peter Fearon, *Origins and Nature of the Great Slump, 1929–1932* (Atlantic Highlands, NJ: Humanities Press, 1979), 34.

23. John Brooks, *Once in Golconda: A True Drama of Wall Street, 1920–1938* (New York: Wiley Investment Classics, 1999), 58–59.

24. "Market Comment," *Wall Street Journal*, 3/21/1928, 22.

25. "Broad Street Gossip," *Wall Street Journal*, 1/13/1928, 2.

26. *Federal Reserve Bulletin* 14:6 (June 1928), 373.

27. John Kenneth Galbraith, *The Great Crash, 1929* (Boston: Houghton Mifflin, 1972), 38.

28. United Nations, *International Capital Movements during the Inter-War Period* (New York: Arno, 1979), 10, table 1.

29. Bernard M. Baruch, *Baruch*, 2 vols. (New York: Holt, 1957–60), 2:218.

30. Richard J. Whalen, *The Founding Father: The Story of Joseph P. Kennedy* (New York: New American Library, 1964), 104.

31. Brooks, *Once in Golconda*, 110.

32. Ibid., 117.

33. "Rockefeller Buys, Allaying Anxiety," *New York Times*, 10/31/1929, 1.

34. Brooks, *Once in Golconda*, 119.

35. Joseph A. Schumpeter, *Business Cycles: A Theoretical, Historical, and Statistical Analysis of the Capitalist Process* (New York: McGraw-Hill, 1939), 2:911.

36. Christina D. Romer, "The Great Crash and the Onset of the Great Depression," *Quarterly Journal of Economics* 105, no. 3 (1990): 606.

37. Fearon, *Origins and Nature*, 34.

38. Robert Skidelsky, *John Maynard Keynes: The Economist as Saviour, 1920–1937*, vol. 2, *John Maynard Keynes* (London: 1992), 391.

39. Herbert Hoover, *Memoirs*, 3 vols. (New York: Macmillan, 1951), 3:2.

40. Whalen, *Founding Father*, 113.

Chapter 2
The Hoover Years

In the spring of 1931 Senator Robert Wagner (D-NY) claimed that President Herbert Hoover had, in the face of crisis, "but clung to the time-worn Republican policy: to do nothing and when the pressure becomes irresistible to do as little as possible."[1] Hoover did not "do nothing," but he did not do enough either. Instead he followed a general policy for crisis management he had already clearly established.

Indeed, when Hoover ran for president in 1928, Americans associated him with competence in a crisis. Some Republican leaders showed skepticism; Calvin Coolidge, whom Hoover served as secretary of commerce, complained, "That man has offered me unsolicited advice for six years, all of it bad."[2] But a new emergency had reminded Americans of Hoover's virtues.

Rains swelled the Mississippi River early in 1927, and in the middle of April the levees near Cairo, Illinois, collapsed. Hundreds of thousands of acres disappeared beneath the water, and more levees burst. Coolidge, who had to this point preferred hopeful inaction, now appointed Hoover to head an emergency committee. A successful mining engineer, Hoover had gone into public service after making his fortune. During World War I, Woodrow Wilson made Hoover head of the effort to provide food and other relief to the war's dispossessed, and Hoover earned a reputation as a logistical genius. "He is certainly a wonder and I wish we could make him President of the United States," Assistant Secretary of the Navy Franklin Roosevelt wrote in 1920.[3] Hoover owed his reputation partly to his talent of organizing and using bureaucracy, and partly to his talent at organizing and using the press. "[T]he world lives by phrases," he once said.[4]

As head of the 1927 flood-relief effort, Hoover showed both the extent and limits of these talents. He organized and managed evacuations, saving lives; he oversaw the establishment of camps to house refugees; he backed federal control of river management to forestall future disasters. Hoover also turned a blind eye as southern whites prevented black evacuees from leaving guarded camps lest the South lose its labor supply. And he used whites' fear to his advantage, threatening local businessmen by saying, "I'll send your niggers north starting tonight," if they did not contribute money to a reconstruction fund.[5]

Like the engineer he was, Hoover could build a machine to solve a problem, but he expected someone else to operate it. He accumulated $13 million in funds for reconstruction loans and made sure everyone knew it, but he did not ensure that the money would get lent to the stricken area, and the vast majority of it was not. Further, although he favored massive federal spending on engineering improvements in river management, he opposed increasing the government's humanitarian role, declaring, "No relief to flood sufferers by Congress is desirable."[6]

As a prospective presidential nominee, Hoover knew he had to promise loyalty and attention to the habitually Republican black voters, without alienating potential white voters. He let African American leaders know he favored a reconstruction plan to subdivide the large farms in the flooded region into small plots for black farmers. But he thereafter declined to support the plan—or the black evacuees—in any substantial way.[7] The flood gave Hoover the ability to claim that he could show grace under pressure. Doubters were few, though sometimes acute: the Baltimore journalist H. L. Mencken wrote that Hoover's "achievements all diminish rather than increase on analysis."[8]

For the 1928 election Hoover's record turned out not to matter much. Hoover won not because of what he had done but because of what his opponent, Al Smith, was: a Catholic. Smith was many other things—most notably, governor of New York, in whose assembly he had also served. New Yorkers knew him as a progressive who had helped reform the state constitution and investigate the infamous Triangle factory fire. Smith had backed bills for workplace health and safety and against child labor.[9] But his accomplishments and Hoover's alike vanished amid a war of symbols waged with Hoover's preferred weapons: phrases. While Hoover kept his distance from the worst slurs, his allies attacked Smith for representing the "sneering, ridiculing . . . foreign-populated city of New York," for opening the way to "card playing, cocktail drinking, poodle dogs, divorces, novels, stuffy rooms, dancing, evolution, Clarence Darrow, overeating, nude art, prize fighting, actors, greyhound racing, and modernism."[10]

What in hindsight looks like a critical election—the choice of a leader for a period of profound crisis—turned on these insubstantial issues of cultural conflict. The election mattered for two major reasons: it left the Republicans in control of government on the eve of the Depression, and it put Hoover, who opposed public relief even in crisis and who believed in the power of phrases to shape the world, in charge of the federal response to economic calamity.

On October 25, 1929, the day after Black Thursday, Hoover told reporters, "The fundamental business of the country, that is the production and distribution of commodities, is on a sound and prosperous basis."[11] Hoover's message was, in the *Wall Street Journal*'s words, "in harmony" with the leading bankers and leading industrialists, who emphasized that "the break ... was a technical one within the market and not based on fundamentals."[12] A few weeks later, Hoover repeated his belief in the soundness of American enterprise, saying, "Any lack of confidence in the economic future or the basic strength of business in the United States is foolish. Our national capacity for hard work and intelligent cooperation is ample guaranty of the future."[13]

Hoover relied heavily on the idea of "intelligent cooperation." He saw himself as cheerleader to American enterprise, not as a referee, coach, or player in the economy: he would call for teamwork and hope to see it produced. He invited important figures in American industry to meet, asking them to reason together, planning how to keep the crash from turning into a depression. He urged employers not to cut wage rates, and they agreed to cooperate.[14] Hoover went further still in his requests, asking state and local politicians to hasten and augment their spending on roads and other public works, believing that in various government treasuries there lay "a substantial reserve for prompt expanded action."[15]

None of these strategies required much action from anyone in the federal government, beyond uttering the occasional encouraging phrase. None provided any immediate relief to Americans. None cost the federal government money. All depended on people outside Washington, DC, to stop the disaster. None worked. The businessmen's pledge to uphold wage rates said nothing about whether they would reduce hours or lay workers off, and they did both. As early as January 1930, *Business Week* reported that "Some automotive companies ... discharged employees with what seemed precipitous haste."[16] Smaller employers, too numerous and minor to get an invitation to Washington, did not feel bound by the wage pledge. Accordingly, unemployment rose and overall wages dropped, even in cases where the nominal rate of pay stayed the same.

Nor were local and state governments able to respond effectively to Hoover's plea. They spent some money on construction projects, but as the crisis continued they had less to spend. Tax revenue fell and the bill for local poor relief rose. These two draining effects on local budgets forced local governments, by the hundreds, to delay, if not repudiate, their debt payments.[17] These government defaults put pressure on another weak pillar in the Hoover plan: his dependence on what he called, in November of 1929, "[t]he magnificent working of the Federal Reserve system and the inherently sound condition of the banks."[18] This assessment proved faulty.

Since beginning operations in 1914, the Federal Reserve System had functioned like a central bank for the United States, regulating the supply of credit in response to economic production. Central banks were supposed also, as the British journalist Walter Bagehot wrote in 1873, to "lend freely" in times of economic crisis, forestalling panic.

But the officers of the Federal Reserve System had not established their own clear set of rules for intervening in crises. Some believed the system must act swiftly to forestall disaster; others thought that the system should keep its credit in reserve unless the need grew truly dire. The balance of opinion within the Federal Reserve rested with the anti-interventionists, as did the balance of opinion within the economic profession during the 1920s. Mostly, economists thought that an economy in crisis should be left alone and that weaker banks and firms should go under. They thought that during a boom period, some businessmen made poor calculations under the influence of excess optimism: they borrowed too much, produced, and stocked too much in anticipation of demand that would never materialize. Economists thought that these poor calculations helped bring on a crisis in the first place, and that the proper role of a downturn was to correct these errors of judgment. As the most popular basic economics textbook of the era said, "The period of depression, then, is one in which ... production is kept at a low level until surplus stocks are disposed of, and new commitments are not made until there is a reasonable assurance of profits. In other words, the period of depression, gloomy and unpleasing as it is, serves as a breathing spell for business[.]"[19]

Moreover, even had economists generally agreed on the need for intervention in time of crisis, the Federal Reserve's officers would have had difficulty knowing just when that crisis had deepened to a point requiring their action. The U.S. government kept no regular statistics on unemployment or on total economic output, nor did it have a system of accounting for national income.[20] Debate among Federal Reserve bankers often rested on anecdotal evidence or assumptions about what was happening in the economy.

In consequence, while in the immediate wake of the Crash the Federal Reserve System took some steps to make it easier for banks to lend and borrow money, after a few months it did little. Some of its members fretted over the relative inaction, noting that the depression seemed to be spreading around the world, particularly afflicting America's debtors. In the spring of 1930, George L. Harrison, governor of the Federal Reserve Bank of New York, visited Europe and observed "a shortage of working capital, and thus a restriction of purchasing power, in a number of countries ... affected by the stringent credit conditions prevailing last year."[21] Harrison believed the Federal Reserve would need to lessen restraints on credit, but a majority of the System's governors disagreed.

The Federal Reserve's caution worked together with the Congress and the president to bring the international economy to a near halt. On June 17, 1930, Hoover signed the Smoot-Hawley Tariff into law, raising taxes on imports to America. The idea for a new tariff bill had arisen in 1928 as a method of protecting American farmers, who were suffering a long bad patch, from foreign competition. By the time it passed, many farmers opposed its provisions, as did newspaper editors, some manufacturing executives, and a number of foreign governments that believed it would cut the American market off from the rest of the world, with dire consequences. Members of the automobile industry, which accounted for 10 percent of American exports, were especially alarmed.[22] A GM executive warned that "a creditor nation ... must, if it hopes to preserve its prosperity ... buy foreign goods of every possible description."[23] Thomas Lamont, a partner in the J. P. Morgan and Company investment bank, claimed he "almost went down on my knees to beg Herbert Hoover to veto the asinine Hawley-Smoot tariff."[24]

But a higher tariff looked to other constituencies like a good idea. Republicans favored tariffs in response to economic complaint. They had used one in the postwar depression of 1921, and it seemed to work then. So they did it again, by partisan majorities—more than 90 percent of House Republicans voted for the bill, more than 90 percent of House Democrats voted against; in the Senate, 78 percent of Republicans were for, and 86 percent of Democrats were against.[25]

The aftermath seemed to prove the critics correct. In the years that followed, other countries retaliated by erecting their own tariff barriers, and world trade fell by one quarter of its volume. Blocking other countries from their American markets made it harder for foreign powers to repay their debts outstanding from World War I. As one writer explained in the *New York Times*, "there is not enough gold in the world to pay America; therefore America must be paid by loans from America and by goods sold in America."[26] With the restriction of credit in 1928, loans from America had begun to fall off, and with the restriction of trade in 1930, goods sold in America began to fall off. Payments to America would have also to fall off, as countries sought to protect their own citizens. Cutting down trade meant cutting down the international flow of borrowed money.

At the end of 1930, the difficulty of borrowing money finally took its toll. In the last two months of the year, bank failures imperiled enormous sums on deposit, more money than suspensions had put at risk in the preceding year.[27] Nor did the panicking end even then; the spasmodic collapse of the American banking system continued. During Hoover's presidency, more than 20 percent of American banks went under.[28]

The American banking system had, contrary to Hoover's assurances, some inherent weaknesses. The laws of many states prevented banks from establishing branch offices. Banks with many interconnected branches, lending money in different places and to different kinds of borrowers, depended less on the fortunes of any single locality and could weather a crisis more easily, while unbranched American banks, or unit banks, failed relatively easily. States that allowed branch banking had stronger, more competitive banks that drove out or absorbed weaker banks. These states entered the Depression with a stronger, more stable financial system. Likewise, the Canadian banking system, with extensive branch banking, survived the Depression largely intact.[29]

The Crash hit American banks hard. Some had made loans to fund speculation; others held foreign assets that went bust, as American loans overseas halted and other countries could no longer meet their obligations. But most important, banks suffered because their clients suffered and could no longer pay off loans or make new deposits in their savings accounts. Payment on loans and new deposits provided banks with their major source of income. As banks' income dried up, they could not pay their own creditors. Increasingly they had to close their doors.[30]

The Federal Reserve System, in keeping with the opinion of a majority of its members that the dying banks were a natural, if painful, part of the circle of life in modern business, did not prevent these failures or forestall further ones. Their inaction accorded with the prevailing orthodoxy of their day. But the prevailing orthodoxy of the 1920s defied the older, and tested, belief set forth by Bagehot in 1873 as well as the evidence before them. Banks continued to fail, in great sickening waves of calamity, each closure sending new ripples of fear far and wide. Americans began to mistrust their banks altogether, which in turn made it still more difficult for banks to get credit.

Much the same could be said of Hoover: while he hewed to the respectable opinion of his day, he defied both the evidence of his senses and a longer-established tradition that cried out for action. And in consequence he too found it harder and harder to get credit as he might have in normal times. Early in October of 1930, Hoover emphasized the psychological causes of Americans' troubles: "The income of a large part of our people is not reduced by the depression ... but is affected by unnecessary fears and pessimism." As to whether the government should take any action, he allowed it might cut the tax on capital gains, which would permit investors to keep more of their profits from trading.[31] A few weeks later, on the anniversary of Black Thursday, Hoover quashed rumors that he would call Congress into special session to take action against unemployment. "No special session is necessary to deal with employment," he declared. "The sense of voluntary organization and community spirit in the American people have not vanished."[32] Hoover's belief in the power of encouraging phrases abided: Americans needed to believe, he thought, in the adequacy of voluntary, civic, nongovernmental action.

A few weeks later, an elite class of Americans lost their jobs all at once: congressional Republicans. In the House of Representatives, the Republicans lost fifty-two seats and yielded control to the Democrats.[33] In the Senate, the Republicans lost eight seats, leaving neither party with a clear majority.

On February 3, 1931, Hoover reiterated his opposition to federal unemployment relief, explaining that he would favor it only "if the time should ever come that the voluntary agencies of the country, together with the local and State Governments, are unable to find resources with which to prevent hunger and suffering."[34] Like the

Federal Reserve, which kept its gold in vaults while banks failed, Hoover would not open the federal treasury for relief until after private and local public institutions collapsed. He opposed federal relief on principle, believing that Americans risked being "plunged into socialism and collectivism" if the federal government provided aid directly to its citizens.[35]

He did not keep faith with cooperative and local efforts entirely in vain. Some businesses tried hard to keep employment stable. General Electric cut back on the number of styles in which it produced lightbulbs, and also committed to fifty weeks of work in 1931 for employees who had been with the firm for two years or more. Some unions worked with their industries to establish unemployment insurance funds. Some companies retrained their workers, in order to ease their movement within the firm. Still others established loans for the unemployed.[36] States did what they could. Governor Franklin D. Roosevelt of New York requested an emergency relief program of the state assembly in the summer of 1931, and Albany responded by devoting $20 million, which went to the relief of more than 300,000 families. Other states followed suit, spending tens of millions of dollars to aid their citizens.[37]

Yet these efforts did not suffice. Consumers spent cautiously when they had no confidence, and hardly at all when they had no jobs. Businesses that depended on consumers' continued confident borrowing suffered. As James Farrell, the president of United States Steel Company, told a congressional hearing late in 1931, "it is difficult to create business beyond the demands of buyers."[38] And as businesses laid off their workers, fewer and fewer consumers had money to spend.

Hoover did not refrain entirely from federal action. In February 1931, he signed legislation creating a Federal Employment Stabilization Board, tasked with timing and scaling federal spending on construction to respond to unemployment.[39] But he supported such laws reluctantly, telling an ally that he preferred "to cut expenses and to give to the country and the world an exhibit of a balanced budget," and he opposed other legislation to expand federal public works.[40] Hoover also ordered stricter enforcement of anti-immigration legislation, and in March of 1931, the *New York Times* reported the White House's claim that "President Hoover, in his efforts to relieve the unemployment situation . . . has kept out of the country nearly 100,000 aliens who would have ben [*sic*] admissible under normal business conditions."[41]

In June 1931, Hoover moved to halt the international propagation of credit collapses, declaring a one-year moratorium on intergovernmental debts. He had his eye particularly on Germany, whose fiscal affairs were sinking ominously. "It is not," the *Times* declared, "that war is threatened there," but rather that "[i]t is today as if there were but a single nervous system for the entire civilized world," and an injury to one extremity affected the whole body.[42]

The moratorium might have delayed a further international financial collapse, but it could provide no immediate relief for Americans. The unemployment rate continued to soar. Retrospective estimates suggest it rose from about 9 percent in 1930 to about 16 percent in 1931 and then to an appalling 23 percent in 1932. During the Depression, government statisticians sensitive to the deepening crisis and wishing to measure its proportions developed the concepts and methods of measuring and defining unemployment that underlie these modern calculations. But their early work produced gloomy numbers, contrary to what the Hoover administration wished to hear and say. The president subjected the chief of the Bureau of Labor Statistics to forcible retirement, as the *New York Times* reported: "'Retired!' he shouted. 'Please don't put it that way. It is not a proper word.'"[43]

In desperation, and in the beginning of his campaign for reelection, Hoover approved a last set of policies for lifting the

Depression. Alarmed by the impending collapse of the California-based Bank of America, Hoover called for emergency legislation to relieve the nation's banks.[44] In January of 1932, he signed into law the Reconstruction Finance Corporation (RFC), capitalized at $500 million and permitted to issue notes of up to $1.5 billion so it could lend money, principally to financial institutions, and thus act (as the Federal Reserve was not) as an energetic lender of last resort and rescue the nation's credit-providing institutions. RFC operated on the theory that if it could ease pressure on banks, eventually they would confer a similar comfort on their borrowers. Within two weeks of its creation, it was making a hundred loans a day.[45]

Hoover also signed a bill allocating $125 million to the Federal Land Bank system, a network of banks established in 1916 to provide farm mortgages. The extra money would prop up the banks in the face of defaulting borrowers and savers who demanded their deposits. Likewise, in the summer of 1932, Hoover signed into law a system of Home Loan Banks to shore up banks that had lent money for homeowners' mortgages. He signed a further bill easing the restrictions on banks within the Federal Reserve System and allowing the Federal Reserve Board greater latitude in manipulating interest rates.[46]

All these measures probably helped loosen restrictions on credit and got bankers and businessmen to lend and borrow more freely again, which might eventually have led to the substantial reemployment of the American people. But they did nothing immediate for non-banker Americans. Hoover's supporters unintentionally damned their own efforts, explaining correctly that they did nothing directly for ordinary citizens. As Secretary of the Treasury Ogden Mills explained, the president's policies "set free the recuperative and constructive forces within business itself . . . so that the nation's business might have an opportunity to do for itself what the Government cannot hope to do for it."[47]

Hoover stood by the principles of relief he had established in 1927—encouraging phrases, widely publicized, and aid to lenders, but no direct assistance to American workers. He disavowed any direct connection to citizens, explaining that he thought the presidency conferred "a power for leadership bringing coordination of the forces of business and cultural life."[48] He left himself entirely open to criticism from Governor Roosevelt, who declared in April of 1932 that "The present administration...has either forgotten or it does not want to remember the infantry of our economic army. These unhappy times call for...plans...that build from the bottom up and not from the top down, that put their faith once more in the forgotten man at the bottom of the pyramid."[49] Roosevelt's speech brought disapproval even from members of his own party, for stirring up the masses against the rich. But by summer he would be the Democratic nominee for president, and in November he would put Herbert Hoover out of work, winning the presidency by a landslide, on the hope that he, as Hoover on principle would not, might bring relief to ordinary Americans.

Notes

1. "Wagner Puts Party in Progressive Role," *New York Times*, 5/15/31, 2.
2. John M. Barry, *Rising Tide: The Great Mississippi Flood of 1927 and How It Changed America* (New York: Simon and Schuster, 1997), 270.
3. Timothy Walch and Dwight M. Miller, eds., *Herbert Hoover and Franklin D. Roosevelt: A Documentary History* (Westport, CT: Greenwood, 1998), 6.
4. Barry, *Rising Tide*, 266.
5. Ibid., 368.
6. Ibid., 401.
7. Ibid., 384–93.
8. H. L. Mencken, *On Politics: A Carnival of Buncombe*, ed. Malcolm Moos (Baltimore: Johns Hopkins University Press, 1956), 148.
9. Robert A. Slayton, *Empire Statesman: The Rise and Redemption of Al Smith* (New York: Free Press, 2001), 98.
10. Ibid., 314, 316.

11. "Hoover Asserts Business Sound," *Wall Street Journal*, 10/26/1929, 1.
12. "Leaders Call Break Technical," *Wall Street Journal*, 10/26/1929, 13.
13. "Text of Hoover's Announcement of Plan for National Conference on Business Aid," *New York Times*, 11/16/1929, 1.
14. Albert U. Romasco, *The Poverty of Abundance* (New York: Oxford University Press, 1965), 29.
15. "Text of Hoover's Announcement," *New York Times*, 11/16/1929, 1.
16. Romasco, *Poverty of Abundance*, 59.
17. Lester V. Chandler, *American Monetary Policy, 1928–41* (New York: Harper and Row, 1971).
18. "Text of Hoover's Announcement," *New York Times*, 11/16/1929, 1. (Capitalization of "system" as in original.)
19. Chandler, *American Monetary Policy*, 119.
20. Ibid., 116.
21. Ibid., 151.
22. Barry Eichengreen, "The Political Economy of the Smoot-Hawley Tariff," NBER Working Paper no. 2001 (1986), 17.
23. "Urge Tariff Cuts to Aid World Amity," *New York Times*, 6/10/1930, 2.
24. David M. Kennedy, *Freedom from Fear: The American People in Depression and War, 1929–1945* (New York: Oxford University Press, 1999), 50.
25. Douglas Irwin, "From Smoot-Hawley to Reciprocal Trade Agreements: Changing the Course of U.S. Trade Policy in the 1930s," in *The Defining Moment: The Great Depression and the American Economy in the Twentieth Century*, ed. Claudia Goldin, Eugene N. White, and Michael D. Bordo (Chicago: The University of Chicago Press, 1998), 334.
26. Edwin L. James, "Peril to War Debts Seen in our Tariff," *New York Times*, 6/18/1930, 1.
27. Ben S. Bernanke, "Nonmonetary Effects of the Financial Crisis in the Propagation of the Great Depression," *American Economic Review* 73, no. 3 (1983): 262.
28. Chandler, *American Monetary Policy*, 105.
29. Mark Carlson and Kris James Mitchener, "Branch Banking, Bank Competition, and Financial Stability," NBER Working Paper no. 11291 (2005); Richard S. Grossman, "The Shoe That Didn't Drop: Explaining Banking Stability During the Great Depression," *Journal of Economic History* 54, no. 3 (1994).

30. Chandler, *American Monetary Policy*, 105–6.
31. "Hoover Asks Bankers to Take Lead," *New York Times*, 10/3/1930, 1.
32. "Work for Jobless Put at $450,000,000," *New York Times*, 10/25/1930, p. 4.
33. Clerk of the House website, www.house.gov, consulted 2/27/2007. The Seventy-first Congress had 270 Republicans and the Seventy-second had 218.
34. "Text of President Hoover's Statement," *New York Times*, 2/4/1931, 2.
35. Joan Hoff Wilson, *Herbert Hoover, Forgotten Progressive* (Prospect Heights, IL: Waveland, 1992), 151.
36. Romasco, *Poverty of Abundance*, 135–38.
37. Ibid., 169–70.
38. Ibid., 139.
39. "Wagner Act Signed by the President," *New York Times*, 2/11/1931, 2.
40. Wilson, *Herbert Hoover, Forgotten Progressive*, 150.
41. "Alien Order Bars 96, 885 in 5 Months," *New York Times*, 3/27/1931, 22.
42. "No Splendid Isolation," *New York Times*, 6/20/1931, 11.
43. "Labor Commissioner Stewart Quits Post," *New York Times*, 7/3/1932, 3.
44. James S. Olson, *Herbert Hoover and the Reconstruction Finance Corporation, 1931–1933* (Ames: Iowa State University Press, 1977), 33–35.
45. Ibid., 42.
46. Romasco, *Poverty of Abundance*, 190–93.
47. Ibid., 197.
48. Ibid., 200.
49. James S. Olson, *Saving Capitalism: The Reconstruction Finance Corporation and the New Deal, 1933–1940* (Princeton: Princeton University Press, 1988), 55.

Chapter 3
Americans in the Depression

The United States endured depressions before the 1930s, but the Great Depression, in its breadth and duration, and in the immediacy of its chronicling, produced also a great compression. The newly interconnected country (Americans in their twenties could remember when there were still western territories, rather than fully fledged states) now had radio and newsreels throughout its towns to show itself how its people suffered. As the Depression lasted, it put the middle class more and more into the circumstances of the poor and encouraged empathy across class lines.

Americans in their forties could remember the last great depression, when the global upheaval of the middle 1890s led to frightening strikes and sent armies of the unemployed tramping the countryside, seeking work they could not find. In the midst of that depression, most voters cast their ballots against William Jennings Bryan, the Democrat who claimed to speak for the downtrodden. But Americans of this generation could remember also how the 1890s fell during an age of globalization, and remembered how so many of the country's workers then had been immigrants, literally of another people. By the Great Depression, this was no longer so true. World War I slowed immigration almost to a halt, and restrictionist legislation of the 1920s pulled America's golden door nearly shut. No longer did the factories seem to teem with newly arrived foreign workers. And so closed one of the gaps that had, a generation before, separated the middling sort from the working class.

The severity of the Depression's misfortune also diminished the distance between the comfortable and the hard-up. So many moved so quickly from one category to another that the employed increasingly identified with their fellow countrymen who were out of work. The gap between income brackets shrank. And where once, not long before, middle-class Americans might reflexively have considered lazy anyone who was unemployed, where once they might have considered radical anyone who claimed the government owed them some assistance, in the 1930s they increasingly saw the suffering millions among them as people much like themselves, who had worked to build the country that seemed now to be falling apart. This diminishing distance between classes helps to explain why Americans embraced E. Y. Harburg's song "Brother, Can You Spare a Dime?", repeatedly played throughout the Depression.

> They used to tell me I was building a dream
> And so I followed the mob.
> When there was earth to plow or guns to bear
> I was always there right on the job ...
> Once I built a railroad, I made it run,
> Made it race against time.
> Once I built a railroad, now it's done
> Brother, can you spare a dime?

As Harburg explained, "This is the man who says: I built the railroads. I built that tower. I fought your wars. . . . I made an investment in this country. Where the hell are my dividends?"[1] Americans who were not themselves out of work—and they were the majority of the workforce—could have ignored this angry and anguished question, as they had at other times in the country's history. But as times got harder, Americans who had something, however little, to spare accepted the justice of the claim, "showering dimes and quarters upon outstretched hands," as the *New York Times* wrote early in 1933.[2] The country that so easily and so recently divided along racial and ethnic lines now drew, even if slightly, closer together.

So quickly after the crash did the crisis grow to such an appalling extent that its full dimensions resisted comprehension. When the unemployment rate ran to around a quarter of the workforce in 1932, about 11.5 million Americans had no work. To put this in some perspective, we might imagine that nearly the entire population of New York, then the most populous state, had no jobs: that from the easternmost tip of Long Island to the shores of Lake Erie, from the Canadian border to Pennsylvania, nobody had work.

But this perspective does not give quite the right picture. Some of the people of New York—children, dependent wives—would ordinarily have held no formal jobs. And the 11.5 million out of work represented only the *workers* who had no paycheck. Many of them had families who depended on them for a living. So the 11.5 million who had no jobs represented something like thirty million Americans who had lost their source of income.[3] Perhaps a quarter of the entire population, therefore, found itself without adequate means to buy shelter or food.[4]

Nor indeed do these numbers, as awful an impact as they make, tell us quite all we should know about the Depression's scope. In unemployment's shadow ran underemployment: those Americans lucky enough to keep their jobs often saw their hours and pay reduced. Employers wanted to keep their skilled workers if they could, so rather than lay people off, they urged their staff to share the burden. To many employees it seemed only fair. And so by the summer of 1932, more than half of American workers did their jobs part-time, keeping on average 59 percent of a full-time job and of full-time pay.[5]

1. These men stand in a New York City breadline in 1932.

Americans in need asked for help reluctantly, and when circumstances forced them to seek help, they went to those closest to them. But in the Depression, each of their customary sources of support failed them, one by one. As a New York City official explained in 1932, "when the breadwinner is out of a job he usually exhausts his savings if he has any.... He borrows from his friends and from relatives until they can stand the burden no longer. He gets credit from the corner grocery store and the butcher shop, and the landlord foregoes collecting the rent until interest and taxes have to be paid and something has to be done. All of these resources are finally exhausted over a period of time, and it becomes necessary for these people, who have never before been in want, to ask for assistance."[6]

When family and neighbors failed, workers could sometimes get help from locally organized mutual assistance funds such as rainy-day plans, or widows-and-orphans money set aside by a union or civic group. Often, Americans set up such plans within their religious or ethnic communities, on the principle of pride, to guard against one of their own having to go to charities or, what felt even more degrading, public relief. So Polish Americans, German Americans, church parishes and congregations, and various other communities kept up aid agencies that tried to provide for the unlucky among them and tide them over until work came. "Let's have pride enough *not* to sponge upon public support when Catholic charity is still able to care for its own interest," one priest declared.[7]

But these networks of support, sufficient to the occasional idle day in a single industry, collapsed under the weight of need that now pressed down on them. So increasingly people turned in shame to public sources of relief, even though it cost them dearly, and sometimes they clung to their self-respect long after they should have, to save their lives, sought help. A doctor working in a free clinic remembered, "The poor got some care, could go to free dispensaries. The rich got good care because they could afford it. There was this big middle class that was not getting any care. The middle class got very much in the position of the poor people.... People of that status would find it very difficult to accept charity.... Every day ... someone would faint on a streetcar. They'd bring him in, and they wouldn't ask any questions ... they knew what it was. Hunger. When he regained consciousness, they'd give him something to eat."[8]

Historically, American cities had through their own treasuries provided relief to their poor, but soon even cities could not help their citizens. In 1932, a Detroit official put it this way:

Many essential public services have been reduced beyond the minimum point absolutely essential to the health and safety of the city.... The salaries of city employees have been twice reduced ... and hundreds of faithful employees ... have been furloughed. Thus has the city borrowed from its own future welfare

to keep its unemployed on the barest subsistence levels.... A wage
work plan which had supported 11,000 families collapsed last
month because the city was unable to find funds to pay these
unemployed—men who wished to earn their own support. For
the coming year, Detroit can see no possibility of preventing
wide-spread hunger and slow starvation through its own
unaided resources.[9]

Sometimes municipal funds might find their way to the needy
through nontraditional routes: in New York, where the Health
Department found that one in five of the city's schoolchildren
suffered from malnutrition, public school teachers, threatened
with pay cuts, paid into a fund from their own pockets for the relief
of their pupils.[10] As civic organizations and governments crumbled
under the weight, often so did families. "A man is not a man
without work," one of the unemployed told an interviewer.[11] Those
men who felt differently—who made for themselves a place in the
world outside the workplace, who as husbands and fathers and
friends and hobbyists knew what was worthwhile to strive for—
shouldered the burden of crisis more easily. But they were in the
minority. As one sociologist wrote, "The average American has the
feeling that work ... is the only dignified way of life.... While
theoretically, economic activities are supposed to be the means to
the good life, as a matter of fact it is not the end, but the means
themselves, that have the greater prestige."[12]

More often than not, men took this sense of duty to heart. They
knew how closely their children watched them, how much hung on
their ability to get even a little work, how much joy it could bring to
a house, or at least how much sorrow it could hold off. As one man
who had been a boy during the Depression remembered,

A lot of fathers—mine, among them—had a habit of taking off.
They'd go to ... look for work.... This left the family at home,
waiting and hoping that the old man would find something. And
there was always the Saturday night ordeal as to whether or not the

old man would get home with his paycheck.... Heaven would break out once in a while, and the old man would get a week's work ... that smell of fresh sawdust on the carpenter's overalls, and the fact that Dad was home, and there was a week's wages.... That's the good you remember. And then there was always the bad part. That's when you'd see your father coming home with the toolbox on his shoulder. Or carrying it. That meant the job was over.[13]

Sometimes men who left to look for work never came back, finding homes in doorways or subways or the communities of shacks on the edges of cities or landfills that, soon enough, Americans learned to call "Hoovervilles." Children who were old enough and independent might themselves leave, foraging on the road instead of relying on overburdened parents. Usually such tramps were young men prepared to fend for themselves, racing to catch boxcars and steal rides. Sometimes the railroad detectives turned a blind eye to their unscheduled human cargo, sometimes not. Sometimes other travelers helped, sometimes they did not. In all, maybe two million Americans made their homes on the road in the years after the Crash.[14]

When employers advertised jobs, they had their pick of workers and could indulge their preferences, or prejudices. Increasingly, they hired or kept on white men with work experience, leaving the young and old, the women, and the African Americans disproportionately represented among the unemployed. Before the Crash, as women first entered the workforce in significant numbers, Americans already found it easy to believe that if a woman worked, she was doing it for frivolous spending money— that properly, women would rely on men who, as heads of households, would supply their wives and children with a living. In the labor glut of the Depression, employers—sometimes by policy, sometimes simply by habit—hired fewer married women and more readily dismissed those they already had on the rolls.[15] Yet women increasingly sought work, mainly to keep families afloat, though sometimes to maintain a middle-class life in the face of the

2. Squatters' shacks populate the banks of the Willamette River in this "Hooverville" settlement near Portland, Oregon.

Depression.[16] Women faced a harder market than their fathers, husbands, brothers, or sons. And if they had to leave their families, life on the road presented an even greater threat of physical exploitation than it posed to their male relations. Accounts of women out of work and without family tell of them establishing communities to protect themselves, sharing meager resources and small rooms, scheduling shifts for the use of beds and clothes. One politician remarked that the woman worker in America was "the first orphan in the storm."[17]

If so, the black worker followed close behind her into the rough weather. In the cities of the United States, African Americans lost their jobs much more quickly than their white counterparts. In part they suffered a misfortune of historical timing: black Americans, long a rural population, had on average moved to cities less recently and had less opportunity to develop careers as skilled laborers than white Americans. But a comparative lack of skills accounted only partially for the high levels of African American unemployment. Black workers noticed that they were "last hired, first fired," and that employers deliberately laid off black workers to replace them with white ones. "So general is this practice that one is warranted in suspecting that it has been adopted as a method of relieving unemployment of whites without regard to the consequences upon Negroes," a National Urban League study concluded in 1931.[18]

These inequities in the job market ensured the Depression-era working class actually in work, or nearest to it, looked much more white, much more male, and overall much more uniform than the working classes of earlier eras. The laborers who held jobs had much visibly in common with one another, and the issues of cultural conflict that so consumed Americans of earlier eras diminished. The object of Americans' solicitude became the imperiled white, male head-of-household, whose hardship they could understand as the nation's concern.[19]

These nationwide hardships crossed the lines between urban and rural populations to an unprecedented degree. Unemployment, as a cyclical problem, had plagued cities as long as there had been cities, and Americans had a folk tradition of returning to the countryside when the cities went into a slump. Farm jobs traditionally enjoyed a resistance to the problems that plagued cities, and in the Depression many Americans did seek out the security of a subsistence farm—in 1932 the farm population rose to the highest point it would reach between the two world wars.[20] But a series of unfortunate events made sure that the countryside suffered the Great Depression as the cities did.

Farm incomes reached their peak around World War I, when the dangers of shipping and general scarcity drove up the price of agricultural produce. High prices inspired farmers to put more land under the plow. Newly available tractors let them do it quickly. Then in the postwar depression, farm prices fell sharply; even after they rose again in the middle 1920s, the prices of the goods farmers had to buy rose higher still. The fresh prevalence of farm machines made it cheaper to produce more agricultural goods on a large scale, and as tractors appeared, mules and men went away. "Tractored out" hands left the countryside to seek opportunity elsewhere.[21] Even the new city prosperity hurt farmers: as urban Americans improved their circumstances, they chose their diets based on taste, rather than need. Once, a wider waistband had signaled health and success, but now thin was fashionable, and food producers' income declined. Further, farmers, like other Americans, took on considerable debt in their expansion and mechanization, rendering them vulnerable to shock.[22]

When the Crash shook this system, the fragile supports for farmers collapsed. Farm income tumbled downward. Creditors forced farmers to sell their property to cover delinquent debt payments.[23] Often, and increasingly, farmers and their neighbors tried to thwart attempts to dispossess them. They might band together and buy property at a delinquency auction, then return it for free to the owner, or they might threaten lawmen who sought forcibly to sell property.

The weather conspired with the man-made calamity. Beginning in 1931, rainfall on the Great Plains lessened until it dropped below the level necessary to sustain crops. Soon the earth would dry and crack so that it could no longer hold itself together, and great winds would simply blow it away.[24]

The South suffered from its continuing peculiarity. Since slavery, its people depended on poorly paid farm jobs to get by. Containing only about a quarter of the nation's population, the South accounted for more than 40 percent of America's farmworkers, and they were the worst-paid hands in the country.[25] Often they were tenant farmers who owed their landlords a share of the crop they produced and had little control over their livelihoods. "In 1929, me and my husband were sharecroppers," one woman recalled. "We made a crop that year, the owner takin' all the crop. This horrible way of livin' with almost nothin'."[26]

As both progress and disaster pushed people off the farms, they left, as able people throughout history have done, seeking better chances. As they did before the Depression, many migrants went West, to California, where the job market might be, and the weather generally was, better. Luckier ones came by car: in 1931, more than 800,000 automobiles entered the Golden State.[27] Less fortunate travelers came by train: in a single month of 1932, the Southern Pacific Railroad company, whose lines ran into and along the length of California, figured it had evicted 80,000 freight-hoppers from the cars it carried.[28] Many of both kinds of migrants wound up encamped throughout California's long valleys, living in tents or small cabins, picking crops for what passed for a living, surviving—or failing to—on beans and rice. Observers figured more than a quarter of the children in such camps suffered from malnutrition, and some of them died of it.[29]

The image of Americans living with almost nothing, driven by drought and storm from their homes, bent under hardship and persevering by will, soon seared itself into the minds of people all over the country. In later years, in reporters' stories and in tales survivors told, in enduring photographs by Walker Evans and Dorothea Lange, and accounts by James Agee and Lorena Hickok, these pictures of poverty in the land of dreamed plenty came to represent the Depression.

But it is worth remembering too that they did not alone represent the Depression, and in the dispassionate view of history, the sudden affliction of the ordinarily affluent may have mattered more. For example, not all the luckless migrants belonged to the chronically poor or even the working class. Many simply found themselves dispossessed as a region's economy succumbed, entire, to the collapse. "We were living in a very large house and making good money," the son of a successful tractor salesman recalled, until "POW—Dad didn't have a job anymore."[30]

As the whole country trembled, if it did not quite crumble, even generally well-off Americans who rarely thought much or concretely about the lot of the poor had suddenly an occasion to think hard on the matter, even though they might not themselves lack work, even though, perversely, the Depression allowed such Americans to live better at lower cost, because sellers in desperation had so lowered their prices. Yet nobody could live quite without worry. They mended their shoe leather with cardboard and stitched pieces of bedsheets together.[31] The recently introduced brand of adhesive cellophane, Scotch Tape, sold well to people trying to fix what they had, instead of buying new.[32]

The crisis developed further, seeming ever more systemic, ever more permanent, and Americans came increasingly to believe that the unfortunate could not, by themselves, bear responsibility for their plight, and that but for the grace of God almost any of the nation's citizens, however prudent and hard-working, might find themselves out of luck one day. And as their own local communities proved inadequate to the catastrophe, they listened increasingly for national voices, which came to them over the radio.

One such voice belonged to Father Charles Coughlin, whose weekly radio broadcasts reached Americans nationwide.[33] Coughlin began his radio career in a parish outside Detroit, taking to the airwaves in the middle 1920s to defy the local Ku Klux Klan. His talents and opinions on a widening variety of subjects won him an ever larger audience. People said you could walk for blocks in

America's cities when Coughlin was on the radio and never miss a word, as the priest's message drifted out his loyal listeners' windows into the street. Speaking over a nationwide network in the Depression, he spoke increasingly about political matters.[34]

Coughlin spoke to a mainly middle-class audience, to people who liked things as they were before the Crash yet who did not own so much that they could insulate themselves from the material or psychological effects of the Depression.[35] Coughlin attacked Communism but, as he told a congressional hearing, he thought the greatest force for Communism in the world was an intransigent capitalist like Henry Ford, who by denying his workers' lesser, reasonable claim for relief risked a revolutionary claim to everything.[36] By 1932, Coughlin and his listeners had reason firmly to put Herbert Hoover in the same intransigent category as Ford. In his last summer as president, Hoover set himself against a new claim for relief from a special category of Americans: war veterans.

In 1924 Congress had voted a special supplementary payment, or bonus, to veterans of World War I based on the length and location of service. The government issued certificates showing the amount owing to each veteran, who could collect either in 1945 or upon his death. As times grew leaner and veterans looked longingly at those sums due in the distant future, they thought perhaps the government might relent and pay them a little early. A bonus due them on their deaths would not do much good, so perhaps they could have it now. After all, Congress had just, at the president's urging, created the Reconstruction Finance Corporation, which would channel as much as $2 billion to banks and railroads to keep them afloat. "If the government can pay $2 billion to the bankers and the railroads," Coughlin wondered, "why cannot it pay the $2 billion to the soldiers?"[37]

Some former soldiers who thought likewise decided to go to Washington, DC, to stake their claim in person. The major, early organization came from Portland, Oregon, but before long news of the movement inspired other marchers, both singly and in groups. Washington police began to prepare for the arrival of twenty thousand men, who became known as the Bonus Army. The Secret Service infiltrated the march to look for threats and found "Generally speaking there were few Communists . . . and they had little effect on the men's thinking. The veterans were Americans, down on their luck, but by no means ready to overthrow their government."[38] On June 7, thousands of soldiers paraded through the city in front of a hundred thousand cheering onlookers.[39]

Others among the capital's defenders assessed the marchers differently. General Douglas MacArthur, then U.S. Army chief of staff, began gathering forces, including tanks, to defend the city against the vagabond threat that began to camp, with the help of city police, across the Anacostia River from the Capitol. Warned repeatedly that they might look like subversives, the marchers policed themselves vigorously, organizing courts and less formal groups to throw out Communists. But it did them no good. Congress adjourned without voting them relief, and the White House and the army grew increasingly concerned the longer they stayed. At the end of July, MacArthur resolved to, in his words, "break the back" of the bonus march with full military force. Soldiers marched out, fixed bayonets, and fired tear gas on the marchers and bystanders alike. Cavalry rode into the crowd; as Major George S. Patton recalled, "Bricks flew, sabers rose and fell with a comforting smack, and the mob ran."[40] Afterward MacArthur claimed he heard, as he generally did, cries of gratitude from the bystanders.[41]

MacArthur's fans, if extant, were surely a minority. Newsreel footage of the clash between the armed and unarmed armies showed tanks rolling through Washington's streets, the veterans' camp burning, and smoke drifting past the Capitol dome. MacArthur and Hoover said they did not believe the men were, in the main, really veterans at all. But the images of American soldiers chasing poverty-stricken Americans petitioning their congressmen elicited the sympathy of viewers. "I felt myself one of them," one woman said.[42]

In Albany, the governor of New York state and Democratic presidential nominee Franklin D. Roosevelt read about the Bonus March in the *New York Times*. Looking at the coverage, he told an aide that they scarcely needed to take Hoover seriously as an opponent after this disaster. Roosevelt said he might feel sorry for Hoover if he did not already feel sorry for the marchers. Indeed, Roosevelt himself did not think the government could afford to pay the men a bonus—indeed, he would veto a bonus bill as president—but, he thought, the men still deserved some sympathetic attention. He thought for a while, smoking. Still, he said, the men making their claim on the government, abused by the administration, "made a theme for the campaign."[43]

Notes

1. William L. Manchester, *The Glory and the Dream: A Narrative History of America, 1932–1972* (Boston: Little, Brown, 1974), 27; Studs Terkel, *Hard Times: An Oral History of the Great Depression* (New York: New Press, 2000), 20–21.
2. "The Lyrical Mr. Harburg," *New York Times*, 1/8/1933, X2.
3. Lester V. Chandler, *America's Greatest Depression, 1929–1941* (New York: Harper and Row, 1970), 34.
4. David E. Kyvig, *Daily Life in the United States, 1920–1940: How Americans Lived through the "Roaring Twenties" and the Great Depression* (Chicago: Ivan R. Dee, 2002), 208.
5. Chandler, *America's Greatest Depression*, 35.
6. Ibid., 41.
7. Lizabeth Cohen, *Making a New Deal: Industrial Workers in Chicago, 1919–1939* (Cambridge: Cambridge University Press, 1990), 218–21.
8. Terkel, *Hard Times*, 145.
9. Chandler, *America's Greatest Depression*, 44.
10. "20.5% of City Pupils Are Found Underfed," *New York Times*, 10/29/1932, 17.

11. Mirra Komarovsky, *The Unemployed Man and His Family* (New York: Arno Press, 1971), 133.

12. Ibid., 82.

13. Terkel, *Hard Times*, 107–8.

14. James R. McGovern, *And a Time for Hope: Americans in the Great Depression* (Westport, CT: Praeger, 2000), 10.

15. Claudia Dale Goldin, *Understanding the Gender Gap: An Economic History of American Women* (New York: Oxford University Press, 1990).

16. Winifred D. Wandersee Bolin, "The Economics of Middle-Income Family Life: Working Women During the Great Depression," *Journal of American History* 65, no. 1 (1978): 70–71.

17. William H. Chafe, *The Paradox of Change: American Women in the 20th Century* (New York: Oxford University Press, 1991), 71.

18. William A. Sundstrom, "Last Hired, First Fired? Unemployment and Urban Black Workers During the Great Depression," *Journal of Economic History* 52, no. 2 (1992): 421.

19. See also Gary Gerstle, *American Crucible: Race and Nation in the Twentieth Century* (Princeton: Princeton University Press, 2001), 177.

20. Susan B. Carter et al., eds., *Historical Statistics of the United States, Earliest Times to the Present, Millennial Edition* (New York: Cambridge University Press, 2006), series Da2; Peter Fearon, *War, Prosperity, and Depression: The U.S. Economy, 1917–1945* (Oxford: Philip Allan, 1987), 176.

21. Kevin Starr, *Endangered Dreams: The Great Depression in California* (New York: Oxford University Press, 1996), 224.

22. Chandler, *America's Greatest Depression*, 56.

23. Ibid., 63.

24. Donald Worster, *Dust Bowl: The Southern Plains in the 1930s* (New York: Oxford University Press, 1979), 11.

25. Kyvig, *Daily Life*, 211; Bruce J. Schulman, *From Cotton Belt to Sunbelt: Federal Policy, Economic Development, and the Transformation of the South, 1938–1980* (Durham, NC: Duke University Press, 1994), 3.

26. Terkel, *Hard Times*, 232.

27. Starr, *Endangered Dreams*, 23.

28. Ibid., 226.

29. Ibid., 229.

30. James N. Gregory, *American Exodus: The Dust Bowl Migration and Okie Culture in California* (New York: Oxford University Press, 1989), 16.

31. Manchester, *Glory and the Dream*, 35.

32. Kyvig, *Daily Life*, 227.

33. Alan Brinkley, *Voices of Protest: Huey Long, Father Coughlin, and the Great Depression* (New York: Vintage, 1983), 92.

34. Ibid., 94.

35. Ibid., 197–98.

36. Ibid., 102.

37. Paul Dickson and Thomas B. Allen, *The Bonus Army: An American Epic* (New York: Walker and Company, 2004), 51.

38. Ibid., 82.

39. "7,000 in Bonus Army Parade in Capital, Orderly but Grim," *New York Times,* June 8, 1932, 1.

40. Dickson and Allen, *Bonus Army*, 176.

41. Ibid., 174.

42. Ibid., 193.

43. Rexford Guy Tugwell, *The Brains Trust* (New York: Viking, 1968), 357–59.

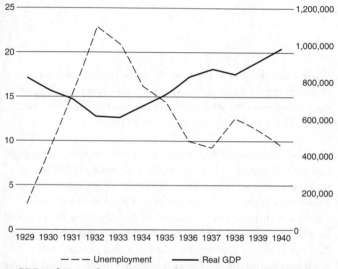

3. GDP and Unemployment. Unemployment as a percentage of the civilian labor force, measured on the vertical axis, and real GDP in millions of 1996 dollars, measured on the right vertical axis.

Chapter 4
Reflation and Relief

When Franklin Delano Roosevelt took the oath of office as president for the first time on March 4, 1933, every moving part in the machinery of the American economy had evidently broken. Banks, farms, factories, and trade had all failed.

Roosevelt right away began working to repair finance, agriculture, and manufacturing, though he would give less attention to overseas economic affairs. As Isaiah Berlin afterward noted, Roosevelt's "great social experiment was conducted with an isolationist disregard of the outside world." The New Deal worked to solve the current crisis and prevent future catastrophe in America alone, by American methods, "with a minimum of relationship with the outside world, which [Berlin continued] was indeed to some degree part of American political tradition."[1]

The Roosevelt agenda grew by experiment: the parts that worked, stuck, no matter their origin. Indeed, the program got its name by just that process: Roosevelt used the phrase "new deal" when accepting the Democratic nomination for president, and the press liked it.[2] The "New Deal" said that Roosevelt offered a fresh start, but it promised nothing specific: it worked, so it stuck.

The administration's policies to revive the money and credit of the country together with its policies to relieve the immediate misery of the American people ranked among the earliest and most enduring successes of the New Deal. From the time of their initial implementation in 1933 to the mobilization for war production in 1940, with the sole exception of the recession of 1937–38, the American economy grew at averaged rates of around 8 to 10 percent a year. Likewise, unemployment fell dramatically from its unconscionable 1932 peak. If merely curing the immediate Depression were the only New Deal goal, its policies of relief and reflation might, pursued vigorously and consistently, have proved sufficient to the task, and their evident success had much to do with the electorate's willingness to support Roosevelt.

Roosevelt began by rescuing the banks. Two days after taking office, he declared the nation's banks must stop transactions in gold, thus shutting them down, and he asked Congress to ratify his action. Congress complied with the Emergency Banking Act on March 9, which affirmed Roosevelt's action, and appointed a receiver with the power to reorganize banks if necessary. In addition, the law empowered RFC to buy bank stock and allowed the Federal Reserve System greater latitude in issuing currency, both measures meant to make money more readily available.[3] Three days later, Roosevelt spoke to the nation over the radio for the first of a series of "fireside chats," in which he explained how the banks worked, what he had done, and that "I hope you can see from this elemental recital of what your Government is doing that there is nothing complex, or radical, in the process."[4] The next day, March 13, banks began to open. Ultimately, the bill allowed about half the country's banks to reopen without qualification, a quarter to reopen with some limits on withdrawals, a fifth to undergo reorganization, and required the remainder—about 1,000 banks—to close up shop.[5]

The bank holiday set a recurring pattern for New Deal legislation. The president would take swift action of sometimes dubious constitutionality—in this case, Roosevelt rested his authority for bank closures on the not transparently applicable Trading with the

4. Franklin D. Roosevelt seated behind a microphone during a
Fireside Chat in 1937.

Enemy Act, passed during World War I and giving the president
powers during war.[6] Congress would quickly comply, often adding
to the bill measures that went further even than Roosevelt
originally anticipated—in this case, not only did Congress amend
the Trading with the Enemy Act to include peacetime emergencies,
it added banking law that drew on preceding state action and on
measures legislators had contemplated during the Hoover
administration. The president would sell the action, with the
charming combination of his aristocratic accent and plain
language, to the American public—in this case, saying simply, "We
had a bad banking situation." Roosevelt would also go beyond
simple folksiness into a teacherly explanation of the circumstances
and his policy, trying truly to explain the technical details of the
emergency and his response. However precipitous Roosevelt's

action, he aimed at fundamentally conservative goals. As one of his advisors, Raymond Moley, later wrote, as a result of the bank holiday, "Capitalism was saved in eight days."[7] Or at least a part of capitalism, anyway. With achievements like this, the crisis in which the country found itself would incrementally improve, earning the administration a degree of credibility and perhaps the latitude for further and lasting reform of the American economic system.

The reform came three months later in the Banking Act of 1933, which owed almost nothing to Roosevelt. The law increased the power of the Federal Reserve Board to regulate banking, divided the banks that dealt with public depositors from those that invested on Wall Street, and—against Roosevelt's initial judgment—established a temporary Federal Deposit Insurance Corporation (FDIC) through which the federal government stood behind the ordinary American's savings. The president worried that the government would one day find itself forced to pay out too large a sum for failed banks, but he accepted the plan—wisely, as it turned out: under FDIC bank failures dropped by an order of magnitude.[8] In 1935 Congress gave FDIC a permanent charter.

In its conservative, capitalism-saving aspect, the story of banking reform adumbrates the later, larger story of the New Deal; throughout, Franklin Roosevelt emphasized his economic orthodoxy. In his radio address he explained that although the Federal Reserve Board could issue more currency now, this currency would rest on a sound basis. "This currency is not fiat currency," he declared. Yet even as he assured the voters, and perhaps himself, of his staid intentions with respect to the currency, he was moving in the opposite direction.

Ever since the 1890s, when the Democratic Party first began to shift from its historic support for limited government, and when, under the leadership of William Jennings Bryan, it began to stand for the ordinary man against the great manufacturing corporations, the Democrats also had a soft spot for soft money.

Bryan stood for the farmer and the worker against the gold standard, adherence to which was driving down the price of agricultural commodities. Instead, Bryan argued, the country should coin silver, inflating—or, properly, reflating—the currency and relieving the downward pressure on prices. Forty years on, the situation looked similar. Roosevelt not only depended on the farm vote, but like Bryan and many if not most Americans, he thought fondly of the nation's long-vanishing family farms, and he hoped to provide them the same relief that Bryan had proposed: more money in circulation, higher dollar prices for their produce, and an easier time repaying their debts. As he said in January 1933, "If the fall in the price of commodities cannot be checked, we may be forced to an inflation of our currency. This may take the form of using silver as a base, or decreasing the amount of gold in the dollar. I have not decided how this inflation can be best and most safely accomplished."[9]

To inflate the currency, Roosevelt would have to cut the dollar loose from gold, to which it, like the other major currencies of the world, had been anchored. Under the gold standard, countries, in theory, agreed to keep their currencies convertible to gold by maintaining only so much money in circulation as their gold reserves warranted. If their gold reserves fell—because, perhaps, their creditors demanded payment—they would have to use their central banks to reduce the money supply within their economies, lest their currencies drop in value. As early as 1929, after the drop-off in U.S. overseas lending and the rise in protective tariffs, the requirement of keeping their currencies in proportion to their gold supplies became too burdensome to a number of Latin American and European countries. The 1931 failure of Credit-Anstalt, a major Austrian bank, led to worldwide gold withdrawals, including from the financial capital of the world, London. By September, Britain had to withdraw itself from the gold standard. To bankers, politicians, and other people who regarded the British empire as solid and the gold standard as the foundation of its solidity, this abandonment looked dire indeed.

In the face of this crisis, the Federal Reserve System raised interest rates to discourage gold withdrawals from the United States. Investors would see the higher rates and know, first, that they could realize a higher return in America, and so keep their money there, and second, that by making money more expensive to borrow, the Federal Reserve meant to reduce the amount in circulation, thus defending the dollar's convertibility to gold.[10] Satisfactory though this strategy might prove to proponents of the gold standard, it made money more expensive at a time when many Americans desperately needed it cheaper. Easier money would have meant more borrowing, more investment, and more jobs. But the system's bankers chose the gold standard over relief of domestic troubles. Hoover made a joint announcement with the French prime minister, Pierre Laval, in support of the gold standard. American central bankers stood with their French counterparts, who "consider[ed] the convertibility into gold not as a servitude which has grown out of date, but as a necessary disciplinary requirement. We see in it the only efficient guarantee for security of contracts and for the morality of business transactions."[11]

The 1933 Emergency Banking Act only temporarily cut the dollar's tether to gold. But in April, Roosevelt issued an executive order preventing Americans from holding gold, except in small amounts, and required them to turn their gold in to Federal Reserve Banks in return for other currency. A few weeks later the president let it be known, the *New York Times* reported, that "He foresaw ... a situation arising where the radical element in Congress ... might ... enact legislation of a revolutionary character"—perhaps to coin silver. To prevent this radical action, Roosevelt allowed that "some sort of inflation might be helpful," but perhaps better that he provide it himself rather than leave it to Congress.[12] It became clear that the temporary escape from gold might represent a new policy entirely. Under the Thomas Amendment to the Agricultural Adjustment Act of May 12, Congress allowed the president to fix the price of the dollar in gold.

The dollar price of gold rose from its previous rate of $20.67 per ounce to $30 per ounce. At the end of the summer, Roosevelt began using RFC to buy gold at steadily higher prices. In a fireside chat he announced, "My aim in taking this step is to establish and maintain continuous control. This is a policy, not an expedient! ... We are thus continuing to move toward a managed currency."[13] In January 1934, Congress passed the Gold Reserve Act, upon which Roosevelt fixed the price of gold at $35 per ounce and took title of all the monetary gold in the country.[14]

The New Deal Congresses reacted to the widespread belief that the bankers and brokers had caused the crash by giving Roosevelt and his appointees extraordinary discretion to manipulate money and banking, which if they had used recklessly might have damaged the financial industry and the American economy. In addition to the Emergency Banking Act and the Thomas Amendment, the Securities Exchange Act of 1934 created the Securities and Exchange Commission (SEC), broadly empowered to regulate Wall Street by preventing traders' misuse of insider information.[15] The Banking Act of 1935 put control of the Federal Reserve System in its board of presidentially appointed governors, rather than in the system's bankers.[16] Roosevelt managed to avoid some of the potential opprobrium from business by judicious use of power and by careful appointments, as when he reassured nervous bankers by appointing veteran trader Joseph Kennedy the first chairman of SEC. Within a few years businessmen gave only SEC among New Deal regulatory agencies a greater than 50 percent approval rating.[17]

Aside from his political judgment, luck also blessed Roosevelt in the use of his broad new powers. When the dollar fell in value, the price of farm commodities, particularly cotton and grain, rose, making it easier for indebted farmers to pay their creditors.[18] Perhaps more importantly, overseas investors began selling their gold for dollars. Gold began flowing into the United States. The

United States had always enjoyed a peculiar position among nations, securely connected to Europe through economic and cultural ties, yet geographically and politically distinct. And now this position began to benefit Americans as political upheaval in Europe, coupled with first the threat and then the actuality of war, increased the golden inflow through the 1930s. This gold put American banks in a much more stable position, increasing the money supply to the American economy. Banks began offering credit at lower interest rates, making it possible for businessmen to consider borrowing and investing in those aspects of their enterprises that would create more jobs, which helped account for the drop in unemployment during Roosevelt's term.[19]

The Roosevelt administration did more than its predecessor to revive American banking, and its efforts evidently succeeded. But the New Deal's financial policies—however plainly Roosevelt explained them over the radio—dealt with matters far removed from ordinary Americans' experience. Later laws did more to put the federal government into the business of backing citizens' investments—the federal government insured mortgages and through dedicated agricultural agencies worked to secure farmers' credit. But in 1933, Roosevelt's policymakers knew they must reach ordinary Americans more directly and quickly than they could by saving banks and stabilizing credit. During the Roosevelt administration, the federal government of the United States began for the first time to offer substantial direct aid to the nation's unemployed. These relief measures emerged piecemeal from political compromises, rather than from blueprints, and changed considerably over the years. The last year of Hoover's administration brought the beginnings of a federal relief program, but it came grudgingly and too slow: the Emergency Relief and Construction Act of 1932 allowed RFC to loan up to $300 million to states for relief. But the program, offering as it did loans rather than grants, and going through existing state bureaucracies, accomplished little and certainly came too late to lift Hoover in public opinion.[20]

Early in the New Deal, congressmen found it easy to identify young unemployed men as especially worth their attention. Young workers, with fewer skills and experience, found themselves out of work more often than workers at the peak of their powers. Yet by virtue of their youth they represented great promise. Young men, by the standards of the era, stood to become future heads-of-household and family providers. Contrariwise, if nobody did anything to help them soon, young men were most likely to leave their communities, becoming tramps or hoboes, posing a threat to social order.

Thus on March 31, 1933, within the first month of the Roosevelt administration, Congress created the Civilian Conservation Corps (CCC), which it chartered initially to provide work for men between the ages of 18 and 35 (inclusive). If single, healthy, unemployed, an American citizen, and a member of a family on relief, a young man could join the CCC, sign over a significant chunk of his wages to his family, and head out for a camp, organized and run by the War Department, somewhere in the American countryside. The Agriculture and Interior Departments had a list of jobs to preserve the nation's crops and forests. Floods and forest fires needed preventing and fighting; pests required eradication; roads and bridges, fences and firebreaks all wanted building. A few hundred thousand of the country's young men, culled from the unemployment rolls and kept to around two and a half thousand camps, supervised by soldiers, seemed just the solution for these problems.[21]

Americans might have worried about CCC's quasi-military qualities and the potential for indoctrination of the nation's youth in government-run camps. But the boys generally served short stints—initial enrollment lasted six months, and legislation later limited enrollment to two years. And as a small, closely focused program justified by generally agreed-upon beliefs identifying young men as especially worthy of the government's resources, CCC enjoyed a comparative freedom from criticism not extended to other New Deal relief programs.[22]

In May, Congress passed the Federal Emergency Relief Act, which created the Federal Emergency Relief Administration (FERA), devoting another $500 million of RFC's money to grants, rather than loans, to the states to support relief. Half the money would go to states based on how much money they themselves spent; the other half relied on the discretion of FERA's administrator. Roosevelt appointed Harry Hopkins, a rail-thin, chain-smoking social worker who ran New York State's relief efforts when Roosevelt was governor, to head the agency. Hopkins set up a desk in a corridor of RFC's offices and began handing out money to the states.[23]

In June, Congress appropriated $3.3 billion, which became the purse of the Public Works Administration (PWA). As the nation's gross domestic product for 1933 amounted only to $56.4 billion, this sum amounted to an extraordinary 5.9 percent of the American economy's overall size that year.[24] Roosevelt appointed his secretary of the interior, Harold Ickes, to run PWA. Originally a Republican from Chicago, Ickes used his vast resources carefully, treating PWA often only as a financing agency for local governments, which had to design, authorize, and appropriate most of the funds to back a major project if they wished to qualify for Ickes's largesse.

In consequence of Ickes's care and Hopkins's comparatively small budget, the early relief effort, even though it earned headlines, made scarcely a dent in the problem of unemployment. Watching as the nation headed into another Depression winter, Hopkins urged on Roosevelt the creation of a new agency, one that would allow him to bypass state officials and employ people directly. Roosevelt obliged by creating the Civil Works Administration (CWA) and charging Hopkins with hiring four million Americans, which he did, by January 1934. Mindful of Americans' attitudes toward public assistance, Hopkins meant CWA to dignify relief by providing work to employees, rather than handouts to clients. Soon CWA workers were fixing up city halls, docks, and public roads, all on the federal government's payroll.

If to Americans of later generations PWA, FERA, CCC, CWA, and RFC, along with their many sibling New Deal agencies, made up a bewildering alphabet soup of bureaucracies, Americans in the 1930s had reason to know which was which. They knew RFC was Hoover's bank-saving agency (now become the pot from which many New Deal agencies scooped a portion), that CCC enrolled their sons and brothers to protect the American land, that PWA would soon build a school, hospital, bridge, port, causeway, or airport (although it had not begun yet), and that CWA got them through the bitter, record-setting cold of winter in 1933/34.[25]

Likewise, the money Congress appropriated for various New Deal programs often later seemed like so many variously sized drops in an ocean of fiscal red ink. In 1932, the federal government spent only about half what the state and local governments spent. By the eve of World War II, the New Deal had more than doubled federal spending. All the while lawmakers, and especially the president, fretted over the millions and billions they added to the federal budget.[26]

Partly for this reason, CWA did not last. Its expense, and even the gratitude with which Americans greeted it, made Roosevelt nervous. He did not like spending more money than the government took in, nor did he like letting Americans rely directly on the federal government for relief programs. In his skittishness Roosevelt conceded the necessity of a national work relief program, but he did not want it to "become a habit with the country." And before spring he had ordered Hopkins to fire his four million workers, in the vain hope that the brief program had provided enough of a push.[27] Despite the phased demobilization of CWA, staggered to prevent too many people from going on the market at once, it left people writing Hopkins plaintively for "some kind of aid a job any where any kind of work" and administrators complaining that a public work half done was worse than one never begun.[28]

66

Despite Roosevelt's nerves, he liked the idea of work relief better than handing out money. So when by the end of 1934 the Depression still had not lifted, his administration began designing a new program of work relief. Americans of the 1930s knew that work relief cost more than direct relief. Simply paying money to the poor was cheaper than setting up a bureaucracy to plan projects to employ the poor. But pride and their morality led them to prefer the costlier course, which allowed desperate Americans the dignity of meaningful work.

The spring of 1935 brought a new Emergency Relief Appropriation Act, giving the president nearly $5 billion for relief projects including highways, conservation, irrigation, electrification, housing, sanitation, reforestation, flood control, and indeed almost any conceivable public good.[29] Roosevelt used the act to set up the Works Progress Administration (WPA), which took over from FERA and became Hopkins's new brief. With WPA, the New Deal government frankly and fully entered the business of hiring the American people to end the Great Depression. Whereas PWA and FERA mostly respected the existing federal structure of the United States, by spending money from the national treasury through state and local governments, WPA repeated and magnified the brief CWA experience, making it an ongoing and central feature of New Deal government.

With WPA, Hopkins once more hired millions, and put them to work building hospitals, schools, playgrounds, and airports. This agency employed artists and writers and actors to ply their trade. It built roads and public housing. but it also drew immediate criticism for spending public money to pay idle hands to do useless work poorly. The purpose and structure of the agency not only guaranteed it would get these complaints, it further guaranteed that such critiques would have some truth in them. Roosevelt meant WPA to hire as many people as quickly as possible to reduce unemployment as much as possible. To really reduce unemployment, its projects could not do what private enterprise was doing, or what local governments were doing; otherwise, the federal government would simply be substituting WPA jobs for already existing jobs and would thus not reduce unemployment. As a result, WPA jobs might well look like the sort of project that would not ordinarily get done—make-work, or boondoggles, or (less ungenerously) the comforts of civilization.

Moreover, WPA offered a temptation for at least mild political corruption. Hopkins had money to give out to local officials, mayors who normally had to beg indifferent or hostile state legislators for support. Now someone in Washington, someone with funds, wanted their friendship. Big-city mayors who governed large voting populations had an especially good claim on WPA's attention.

Congress responded to concerns about WPA's possible political uses by drawing ever-narrower boundaries around the agency, boundaries that by themselves indicate what worried or offended people about the agency. From 1936, illegal immigrants could not work for WPA. From 1937, WPA workers had to accept private-sector offers or be released from the agency. From 1938, WPA employees had to supply a quarterly statement of outside earnings, if any; veterans had first right to a WPA job, then American citizens, then immigrants who had declared an intent to become citizens. Other immigrants could not apply. From 1939, workers could stay on the rolls for only eighteen months unless recertified as needy, and WPA workers had to be American citizens.[30]

While Congress tried to prevent the political use of WPA, criticism of its projects backfired. Public works that might look extravagant at first glance (a $25,000 dog pound for Memphis, Tennessee, for example) turned out to serve a useful purpose, reducing the number of dog bites and treatments for rabies in the city.[31] Each project proved popular in its own community. And WPA built a great many projects.

On the whole, WPA embodied new assumptions about earnings. It defined a "security wage," which though minimally adequate was often higher than private bosses wanted to pay, and its paychecks came with a regularity previously unknown to workers accustomed to seasonal or cyclical unemployment. It contributed legitimacy to the once unorthodox idea that Americans deserved a certain degree of job security and a minimum standard of living as an essential part of their dignity. Americans, WPA's "security wage" suggested, ought to earn a wage sufficient to provide them more than subsistence, enough to allow them pride and independence from their employers.[32]

A 1939 Institute of Public Opinion poll found that, when asked to name "the worst thing the Roosevelt Administration has done," 23 percent of Americans picked "Relief and the WPA," making it the most unpopular New Deal measure. Given the American prejudice against federal relief and the potential for political abuse, it was scarcely surprising. The same poll found that, when asked to name "the greatest accomplishment of the Roosevelt administration," 28 percent of Americans picked "Relief and the WPA," making it the most popular New Deal measure. Given the variety and local popularity of relief projects, this was unsurprising too. That 5 percent margin on an issue central to the New Deal made more than enough political difference to the Democrats.[33]

Between the immediate effects of relief, which gave Americans not just something to spend, but the ability to regard themselves again as decent and productive citizens, and the longer-term effects of reflation, which quietly began rebuilding the private-sector economy, the Roosevelt administration might have had an adequate strategy for fighting the Depression, although for the government really to pull the country out of its economic slough would require a more vigorous pursuit of both policies. But its policymakers wanted to accomplish something further and different than the mere conclusion of a crisis: they wanted to make sure the Depression could not happen again. To do so, they expected to change the American political economy forever.

Notes

1. Isaiah Berlin, "President Franklin Delano Roosevelt," in *The Proper Study of Mankind: An Anthology of Essays*, ed. Henry Hardy and Roger Hausheer (London: Chatto and Windus, 1997), 629.
2. William E. Leuchtenburg, *Franklin D. Roosevelt and the New Deal, 1932–1940* (New York: Harper Torchbooks, 1963), 8.
3. James Stuart Olson, *Saving Capitalism: The Reconstruction Finance Corporation and the New Deal, 1933–1940* (Princeton: Princeton University Press, 1988), 30.
4. First Fireside Chat (Banking), May 12, 1933, consulted online 2/27/2007, www.presidency.ucsb.edu/ws/index.php?pid=14540.
5. Peter Fearon, *War, Prosperity, and Depression: The U.S. Economy, 1917–1945* (Lawrence: University Press of Kansas, 1987), 219.
6. Samuel Anatole Lourie, "The Trading with the Enemy Act," *Michigan Law Review* 42, no. 2 (1943).
7. Raymond Moley, *After Seven Years* (New York: Harper and Brothers, 1939), 155.
8. Milton Friedman and Anna Jacobson Schwartz, *A Monetary History of the United States, 1867–1900* (Princeton: Princeton University Press, 1963), 437.
9. Barrie A. Wigmore, "Was the Bank Holiday of 1933 Caused by a Run on the Dollar?," *Journal of Economic History* 47, no. 3 (1987): 743.
10. Lester V. Chandler, *American Monetary Policy, 1928–41* (New York: Harper and Row, 1971), 177.
11. Ibid., 168.
12. "President's Action Forced by Events," *New York Times*, 4/20/1933, 1.
13. Chandler, *American Monetary Policy*, 276.
14. "President's Statement of Action under the New Law," *New York Times*, 2/1/1934, 12; Gold Reserve Act is 48 Stat. 337; Friedman and Schwartz, *Monetary History*, 465.
15. 48 Stat. 881.
16. Richard H. Timberlake, *Monetary Policy in the United States: An Intellectual and Institutional History* (Chicago: University of Chicago Press, 1993), 283.

17. Ralph F. de Bedts, "The First Chairmen of the Securities and Exchange Commission: Successful Ambassadors of the New Deal to Wall Street," *American Journal of Economics and Sociology* 23, no. 2 (1964): 176.

18. Christina D. Romer, "Why Did Prices Rise in the 1930s?," *Journal of Economic History* 59, no. 1 (1999): 174.

19. Romer, "What Ended the Great Depression?," *Journal of Economic History* 52, no. 4 (1992): 757.

20. Lewis Meriam, *Relief and Social Security* (Washington, DC: Brookings Institution, 1946), 346.

21. Ibid., 434–42. Also Neil M. Maher, *Nature's New Deal: The Civilian Conservation Corps and the Roots of the American Environmental Movement* (New York: Oxford University Press, 2007).

22. Meriam, *Relief and Social Security*, 441–42.

23. Leuchtenburg, *Franklin D. Roosevelt*, 120–21.

24. *Historical Statistics of the United States*, Millennial Edition Online, series Ca74.

25. Leuchtenburg, *Franklin D. Roosevelt and the New Deal*, 122.

26. *Historical Statistics of the United States*, Millennial Edition Online, series Ea18.

27. Leuchtenburg, *Franklin D. Roosevelt and the New Deal*, 122.

28. Bonnie Fox Schwartz, *The Civil Works Administration, 1933–1934: The Business of Emergency Employment in the New Deal* (Princeton: Princeton University Press, 1984), 234.

29. Meriam, *Relief and Social Security*, 354–56.

30. Ibid., 380–82.

31. Jason Scott Smith, *Building New Deal Liberalism: The Political Economy of Public Works, 1933–1956* (Cambridge: Cambridge University Press, 2006), 149.

32. Meriam, *Relief and Social Security*, 385.

33. "Relief Top Issue, Survey Indicates," *New York Times*, 6/4/1939, 27.

Chapter 5
Managing Farm and Factory

The New Deal's earliest efforts to rewrite the rules of the United States' political economy included two major agencies to centralize the planning of American production. Both efforts had more to do with ambitions dating back to World War I than with responses to the current crisis. And major components of both efforts failed politically, but in their failure they pointed the way to a different policy for preserving American capitalism.

If American money and banking policy put the United States on the road to recovery within the first year of the Roosevelt administration, it did little to help stabilize the world economy. Indeed, as American monetary policy brought gold into the United States, other countries felt pressure as their money supplies dwindled. Roosevelt made it amply clear in his first year that he could spare no thought for other countries as long as the American situation remained so dire. In the summer of 1933 he scuttled the international London Economic Conference by sending the message, "The sound internal economic system of a Nation is a greater factor in its well being" than anything the conference could decide.[1] The peoples of the rest of the world would have each to find their own route out of the crisis.

Some countries left the gold standard and began groping their own way back to prosperity, in some cases by establishing exclusive trade relations within their old colonial empires. Everywhere, falling commodity prices hit farmers cruelly hard, and many colonized countries had few major occupations besides farming. Colonies, as ever, found themselves at the mercy of their imperial masters. Latin American countries sought bilateral trade arrangements to ensure purchases, Brazil offering coffee for German machinery and Argentina selling beef to Britain.

As the crisis continued, political parties gained support by proposing radically new systems of social organization. Fascist and Communist movements gathered strength by promising various forms of state socialism that would control national economies and restore stability. Anti-imperialist movements arose to promise independence to beleaguered farmers in the colonized world.[2] Everywhere, people hurt by the Depression sought some new form of society immune to the ailments they faced. Or almost everywhere: while the United States experienced some of the same pressures, and sometimes its sufferers saw themselves in similar terms to their peers in other countries, its radical movements looked more traditional than novel. For example, one American farm advocate declared that "American agriculture stands in just the same subservient position to American industrialism that the colonies occupied toward England a century and a quarter earlier."[3] But unlike their similarly economically subservient colonial cousins, American farmers had representation in their legislature—indeed, more representation than their numbers alone would merit. In consequence, although the New Deal included American experiments with economic planning, the tactics adopted had less to do with radical responses to the immediate crisis and more to do with the long history of farm grievances in America.

By the time the United States sank into the Great Depression, the country had already seen seventy years of nearly constant agitation for federal action in favor of farmers. The legislation of the Civil War era—principally the Homestead Act, the Pacific Railroad Act, the Morrill Land Grant Act—encouraged Americans to go West in the belief they would there find land on which they could settle into single-family farming. The Reconstruction of the South after the war had, albeit briefly, encouraged similar hopes of establishing more single-family farms there. But small-time farmers in America came soon to grief, suffering various combinations of aridity, debt, infestation, and the consolidation of farmland in fewer, larger holdings.

As one economic history of the United States has it, "Farmers are always unhappy."[4] "Always" may slightly overstate the case, but even so, a variety of factors conspired to keep farmers on edge for almost the entirety of the early twentieth century. Expensive and innovative technologies made farming less a family pursuit and more an industrial concern, with sound credit and efficiency surpassing diligence and hardihood as the cardinal agrarian virtues. The extension of transportation networks throughout the world put farmers ever more obviously into competition with an international market. Even as farmers faced more overseas competition, they saw American tariff policy protect their fellow citizens in manufacturing from the same pressures: for much of this period, Congress favored using import taxes to prevent foreign factories from selling their goods in the American market. Behind the shield of the tariff, farmers saw, American manufacturers could reduce production and raise prices without fear of international competitors undercutting them. Meanwhile, the American people moved in droves to cities, putting urban life and concerns at the center of national debate and relegating agriculture to the margins.

While farming dwindled in economic and cultural importance, farmers retained an outsized influence on national politics. Because the United States Senate allocates legislators to states, not to people, it overrepresents the less populated, more heavily agrarian states of the nation. In consequence, farmers retained great, though waning, influence in national politics even as they became fewer in number. Further, Congress's failure to adopt a

redistricting scheme after the 1920 Census—the first
count that showed more Americans living in cities than on
farms—guaranteed that rural Americans enjoyed better
representation in the House of Representatives than their
numbers warranted.[5]

Into the 1920s, the effects of World War I rendered more acute the
chronic unhappiness of American farmers. During the war, the
United States shipped meat and grain to its allies, rationing them
at home on wheatless and meatless days. Thus deprived of their
traditional diet, Americans learned to eat more of the more
perishable fruits and vegetables, which also—Americans
found—kept them healthier. Also, the passage of laws prohibiting
manufacture and sale of alcoholic drinks reduced consumption
of grain. Thus demand for the staples of the American farm fell.[6]

At the same time, farmers increased their harvests. While the
European powers waged war, American farmers rushed to feed
them, turning fields over to grain that might otherwise have lain
fallow or served as pasture. When the war ended, this extraordinary
demand ceased, but American farmers generally kept up their new
levels of productivity in the hope that prosperity might return.[7]
With decreased demand and increased supply, farm prices fell.
They might have risen again if enough people left farming for other
pursuits and turned their land over to other uses. But many
American farmers wanted to remain farmers; they just wanted to
become better paid ones. So they banded together to lobby for
legislation restoring them to parity with their fellow countrymen in
the cities. They wanted to stay on the farm but live as comfortably as
people who worked in offices and factories. And increasingly, they
pointed to the era just before World War I as their golden mean,
when farm goods fetched what they saw as a fair price.

To return to that period of parity, farmers believed, they would
have to arrange their economic activity much as manufacturers
did, which meant controlling prices by curbing production. As

75

Henry A. Wallace, who would serve as secretary of agriculture under Franklin Roosevelt, said in 1922, "It is no more wrong for farmers to reduce production when prices are below cost of production than it is for the United States Steel Corporation."[8] To Wallace and his allies, U.S. Steel symbolized all industrial corporations that enjoyed advantages farmers did not: the tariff protected manufacturers from foreign competition, and the scale and scope of their operations let a central office reach decisions that swayed the entire domestic market. Providing similar benefits to agriculture meant first of all, as one advocate put it, "getting the tariff to the farmer."[9] But just blocking imports with a tariff would have done no good, as American farmers were already producing far more than the domestic market could consume. So farmers needed further methods of gaining benefits similar to those enjoyed by industry. In addition, farmers could only pine for the centralized efficiency of major corporate offices: farm producers were too many and too scattered to decide on concerted activity.

In the early 1920s, farm advocates sketched a plan to skirt these obstacles. George Peek, president of the Moline Plow Company in Illinois, along with his business partner, Hugh S. Johnson, realizing "you can't sell a plow to a busted farmer," developed an idea that the farm bloc in Congress supported. Peek and Johnson had both worked with the War Industries Board (WIB), the agency that regulated American production during World War I, and they believed their experience of managing an economy almost totally sealed off from the world market would suit the country now. A tariff, they thought, should block imports of farm goods, and a government corporation should buy up any crop surplus and seek to export it overseas. Farmers' marketing associations would work to coordinate domestic production. Peek's plan became the basis for the McNary-Haugen bills passed by Congress in the late 1920s and vetoed by President Calvin Coolidge on the grounds that they would interfere too much with the free market and raise prices for urban consumers. During his presidency, Herbert Hoover

sought a halfway position; even before the Crash he backed
Congress's 1929 creation of a Federal Farm Board empowered to
loan money to farmers and to store excess crops, while encouraging
cooperative action in American agriculture. Like other Hoover
policies, it proved unequal to the Depression.[10]

Other farm advocates pushed the McNary-Haugen idea further,
believing that tariff-like protections would not work well enough;
farmers had also to reduce their production. W. J. Spillman, an
economist working for the Department of Agriculture, developed a
plan of "domestic allotment." Examining the domestic
consumption of (for example) wheat, the government would
determine the size of the domestic market for a commodity and
allot to each state and farm an appropriate share of this market.
Farmers producing their allotted share would receive market value
plus a bonus for their crop, and would have to take only market
value for any further production.[11] Milburn L. Wilson, a professor
of agricultural economics at Montana State College, promoted
domestic allotment aggressively, adding to the original idea and
urging it on farm association and broader business interests alike.
In its mature phases, the plan included self-financing provisions,
taxing the processors of a commodity (e.g., millers of grain into
flour) to pay for the allotments. Wilson promoted this plan to
Roosevelt's campaign in 1932, and Roosevelt spoke favorably of an
interventionist farm policy in (as his advisor Raymond Moley said)
"generalities too vague to require examination."[12]

The New Deal's first major farm legislation, the Agricultural
Adjustment Act of 1933, reflected this long, if mixed, lineage.
Although it began by citing "the present acute emergency," it
focused on farmers' longer-standing complaints. It charged the
government with erasing the "severe and increasing disparity
between the prices of agricultural and other commodities, which
disparity has largely destroyed the purchasing power of farmers,"
and it specifically pointed to the years just before the deranging
effects of World War I as the ideal of parity to which the country

should return. And in keeping with the New Deal preference for vague generalities, it left the exact mechanism of the plan up to the president but provided him the powers to reduce acreage under production, to pay benefits for desirable harvests, and to tax processors, all of which the domestic allotment idea required.[13] In addition, the law exempted farm associations from antitrust prosecution (making it possible for farmers to centralize their decision-making) and made participation in its programs voluntary.

Roosevelt's appointments also reflected the heritage of his farm policy: he named Wallace as secretary of agriculture and Peek as head of the new Agricultural Adjustment Administration (AAA), which would administer the production-control policy. Wilson became head of AAA's wheat section.[14] Differences of opinion split these three longtime lobbyists for federal farm policy; Peek preferred the use of marketing associations to reducing production, Wilson wanted the domestic allotment plan as a step to permanent acreage reduction, and Wallace told Wilson the programs might work "if we are really going the route of state socialism. And I am very much inclined to think that we really are going that route."[15] Coupled with the vagueness of the law and of Roosevelt's wishes, these divisions made an already difficult job harder.

By the time AAA got under way in the spring of 1933, cotton growers had already planted their crop. Seeing an abundance of cotton already on hand, AAA asked growers to plow up their plants in exchange for a fee, lest already low cotton prices fall further. AAA agents spread out over hundreds of counties to persuade farmers to dig up what they had just sown. They met problems typical to any bureaucracy—they never had enough blank contract forms where they needed them, and farmers complained about the fairness of yield estimates, and an estimator's freedom to indulge his friends: "Our estamater sure did not give us a fair deal.... He has pets."[16] Checks for the plow-up often came late.

Beyond these ordinary administrative difficulties, AAA met problems specific to its agrarian mission. Mules long-trained to avoid plowing up cotton plants balked when set to the task. Poor weather prevented plow-ups in some places, and fair weather discouraged farmers from plowing up a good crop in others. Sometimes a sheriff had to send a tractor to enforce a plow-up contract and charge the cost to the reneging farmer.[17] When plow-up checks did come, landlords sometimes kept the payments from tenants.

If the spectacle of a government destroying cotton when millions of its people went without adequate clothing rankled, the spectacle of that government destroying food in the midst of hunger positively hurt. But to keep hog farming incomes up to parity, AAA officials decided they had to slaughter millions of piglets, lest they in future years fuel a glut. "That we should have . . . idle and hungry and ill-clad millions on the one hand, and so much food and wool and cotton upon the other that we don't know what to do with it, this is an utterly idiotic situation, and one which makes a laughing stock of our genius as a people," a Missouri farm leader claimed.[18]

5. These men, members of the Civilian Conservation Corps, worked on a poultry-raising farm in Jonesville, Virginia.

None of the farm policy's architects really meant it to address the nation's ancient problems of rural poverty or the new problems of the Great Depression. The law specifically aimed to erase the inequality in purchasing power between countryside and city by moving back to an imagined golden age, not forward to a brave new world. Far from stimulating recovery by aiding the majority of the nation's buyers, its regressive processing taxes, passed on to consumers, penalized urban buyers to benefit rural sellers.

Farmers mainly supported such policies: cotton growers lobbied to have acreage reduction made compulsory once they realized that nonparticipating farmers would derive the benefits of raised prices without having to sacrifice a portion of their crop. In response Congress passed the Bankhead Cotton Control Act of 1934, taxing farmers on everything they sent for ginning over their quota. This law required a referendum after its first year of operation, and in the vote almost 90 percent of cotton-growers nationwide favored its retention.[19]

As John D. Black, an economist sympathetic to the domestic allotment plan, noted in 1936, AAA took for its goal a relative rise in farm incomes, not a rapid recovery from the Depression. For a speedy recovery, a policy of raising farm incomes was generally thought inferior to a policy of raising business profits, because business profits meant more investment and higher wages for more consumers. The best case one could make for AAA, Black wrote, was "that it has given us a *better* recovery than would a business-profits recovery, because . . . it has given us a *better distributed* recovery"—which was to say, a recovery better distributed geographically, from city to farm, not a recovery better distributed across classes. And even that case did not hold up especially well, Black noted: while farm prices had risen, perhaps two-thirds of their rise owed to drought and to the devaluation of the dollar rather than to AAA action.[20] Moreover, as much as farmers liked the rise in their prices, they lamented a simultaneous rise in the prices of the goods they bought—a rise they attributed to the New Deal's other major economic management law, passed a month after the agriculture act.

Industrial policy, like farm policy, drew on an established tradition of centralizing authority to control prices, harking back to a perceived golden era—this time during World War I, when the government worked with business leaders on WIB to encourage cooperation and command of production. While WIB veteran George Peek went to head AAA, his old colleague from WIB days, Hugh Johnson, helped create and run its industrial counterpart, the National Recovery Administration (NRA).

At least since the great merger movements of the late nineteenth century, major American businessmen regarded with suspicion the principle of unfettered competition, which lowered the prices they could get for their goods and services, sometimes below the cost of production. Increasingly, they professed to believe in an " 'economic right price,' the 'universal use' of which, through federal regulation, 'would wholly and permanently eliminate unfair price-cutting.' "[21] Businessmen thus faced similar problems to American farmers, while enjoying certain natural advantages. Manufacturing lent itself to centralized control more easily than farming. Innovation in technology and techniques permitted ever greater substitutions of machine and management efficiency for employment of skilled labor, and thus put control of the factory floor more securely into the hands of businessmen. Indeed, perhaps the only obstacle (however low) to the utter concentration of manufacturing was the federal antimonopoly code.

WIB taught businessmen that with government cooperation, instead of antagonism, they could control production to fix prices, prevent strikes, and make a decent profit—all while appearing patriotic. The Depression afforded them an opportunity to lobby once more for such an emergency arrangement so they could determine the right, higher price for their products.

The first business-government collaboration of the Depression had been the Hoover-era "Buy Now" campaign. Journalists, politicians, and other boosters implored the consumers who had driven the boom of the 1920s to purchase their way back to prosperity. This rhetorical campaign failed. In 1931 *Business Week* reported, "The 'Buy Now' idea seems to have faded out.... There appears to be increasing doubt as to what buyers should use for money."[22] By the Roosevelt administration, it had become clear it would require more than cheerleading to increase purchasing power. Roosevelt asked his secretary of labor, Frances Perkins, if she could come up with a way to provide labor unions a place in the industrial policy for reducing competition. Perkins, America's first female cabinet member, had served in Roosevelt's New York administration, where she advocated minimum wage and maximum hours legislation. Now she proposed the creation of industrial boards, on which representatives of management, labor, and the government might sit together. To participate in the policy, unions would also need a right to organize, which Supreme Court cases had questioned even after the 1914 Clayton Act exempted unions from the antitrust laws. The American Federation of Labor (AFL) defended the right to organize as a way to increase "buying power."[23]

An economist with the brand-new AAA argued that the industrial legislation had to perform a similar purpose to the farm law—to promote not a speedier, but a better distributed, recovery: "I think the act has got to do something about improving wages, about improving labor conditions, about protecting collective bargaining so that it will be in better balance, and so we will have a stimulation of consumer interest and consumer buying."[24]

Like the Agricultural Adjustment Act, the industrial legislation reflected its mixed origins. The National Industrial Recovery Act of 1933 included a variety of measures, including provision for public works that allowed Roosevelt to create his work-relief agencies. But its major provision allowed the creation of a more managed industrial policy through boards like the ones Perkins had envisioned, with management, labor, government, and consumer representatives negotiating regulatory codes. Congress suspended the antitrust laws to permit price-fixing among businesses for a two-year period. It authorized the president to set, or to delegate authority to set, codes of operation for industry that would determine the basis for fair competition. In section 7a of Title 1, the law required such codes to guarantee that

> employees shall have the right to organize and bargain collectively through representatives of their own choosing, and shall be free from the interference, restraint, or coercion of employers of labor, or their agents, in the designation of such representatives or in self-organization or in other concerted activities for the purpose of collective bargaining or other mutual aid or protection.[25]

Unions, business groups, and consumer advocates waited to see what the President would do with his new powers.

Roosevelt launched NRA with warlike rhetoric, invoking "the great cooperation of 1917 and 1918" as precedent, and named Hugh Johnson, the former general, to run it, thus satisfying the businessmen who looked fondly to WIB for inspiration. Johnson created a martial symbol for NRA, a blue eagle clutching a gear and a clawful of thunderbolts. He tried to mobilize consumers by extending the wartime metaphor. "It is women in homes and not soldiers in uniform who will this time save our country.... It is zero hour for housewives."[26]

The price-raisers had the upper hand because executives of large corporations had more control over their enterprises, greater familiarity with the scale and scope of their operations, and a good friend in Hugh Johnson. By the end of summer 1933, most major industries had developed codes, while less than 10 percent of the industries with NRA code-making authorities had a labor member and even fewer had a consumer representative. Thus, many of the codes resulted from negotiations between businessmen and government officials, many of whom had recently been businessmen themselves. As one observer complained, NRA codes looked like "a bargain between business leaders on the one hand and businessmen in the guise of government officials on the other."[27] Labor leaders discovered that management could circumvent section 7a by creating company-run unions. Workers began to complain that prices were going up, but not wages. NRA, which looked every day more like what critics called an "Old Deal" organization, repeated the Hoover-era "Buy Now" campaign, to the same response: "What with?" as one farmer asked.[28]

NRA also deeply vexed some owners of smaller businesses. Many found themselves ill-equipped to deal with the bureaucratic requirements of code compliance and unlikely to make themselves heard against larger competitors in the code-making authorities. The principal price-fixing measures of the codes catered to larger businesses trying to prevent niche competitors from undercutting them. And especially in the Depression, standing up for the little guy offered an irresistible political opportunity, as Frances Perkins observed: "You can always get sympathy by using the word small. . . . With little industries you feel as you do about a little puppy."[29] In response NRA established a board to investigate such complaints. Headed by the celebrity lawyer Clarence Darrow, the study discovered "monopolistic practices" in seven of the eight NRA industries it studied, and found that small businesses were "cruelly oppressed."[30]

By 1934, NRA had stalled amid criticism. Johnson resigned, replaced by a committee. Early in 1935, an examination of NRA found only two instances in which codes had been enforced against business. With the two-year exemption from antitrust prosecution nearly expired, the Senate defied Roosevelt, voting only a limited extension of NRA.[31] Before the House could decide whether it agreed, the Supreme Court declared NRA unconstitutional—but it was already clear that in Roosevelt's subsequent, privately expressed opinion, NRA gave him "an awful headache" and some of its policies had been "pretty wrong."[32]

Before long the Supreme Court would also strike down AAA. For the Court, the two agencies similarly violated the Constitution: they exerted an unprecedented and unauthorized coercive executive power within states. As Henry Wallace had said, such agencies edged toward "state socialism," which it is fair to suppose most Americans, even in that desperate crisis, regarded with suspicion.

Shorn of their more statist, managerial elements, key parts of the AAA and NRA survived as Congress reenacted them in law. Inasmuch as neither program aimed at a swift recovery, but tried instead to provide a different balance in the distribution of American wealth and power—from city to countryside and from management to labor and consumers—the policies enjoyed considerable popularity among important Roosevelt constituencies, representing aspects of the New Deal approach to political economy that would last well beyond the Depression.

Notes

1. Lester V. Chandler, *American Monetary Policy, 1928–41* (New York: Harper and Row, 1971), 281.
2. Dietmar Rothermund, *The Global Impact of the Great Depression* (London: Routledge, 1996), 107, 29.
3. Judith Goldstein, "The Impact of Ideas on Trade Policy: The Origins of U.S. Agricultural and Manufacturing Policies," *International Organization* 43, no. 1 (1989): 35.
4. Susan Previant Lee and Peter Passell, *A New Economic View of American History* (New York: W. W. Norton and Company, 1979), 301.
5. Zechariah Chafee Jr., "Congressional Reapportionment," *Harvard Law Review* 42, no. 8 (1929); Orville J. Sweeting, "John Q. Tilson and the Reapportionment Act of 1929," *Western Political Quarterly* 9, no. 2 (1956).

6. Theodore Saloutos, *The American Farmer and the New Deal* (Ames: Iowa State University Press, 1982), 9.

7. Ibid., 5.

8. Ibid., 32.

9. Goldstein, "Impact of Ideas," 43.

10. Keith J. Volanto, *Texas, Cotton, and the New Deal* (College Station: Texas A&M University Press, 2005), 15 ff.

11. Ibid., 20.

12. William D. Rowley, *M. L. Wilson and the Campaign for the Domestic Allotment* (Lincoln: University of Nebraska Press, 1970), 15; Saloutos, *The American Farmer and the New Deal*, 41; Volanto, *Texas, Cotton*, 22.

13. 48 Stat. 31, 34–5.

14. Rowley, *M. L. Wilson*, 195.

15. Ibid., 138.

16. Volanto, *Texas, Cotton*, 45.

17. Ibid., 49.

18. Anthony J. Badger, *The New Deal: The Depression Years, 1933–40* (London: Macmillan, 1989), 163.

19. Volanto, *Texas, Cotton*, 83.

20. John D. Black, "The Agricultural Adjustment Act and National Recovery: Discussion," *Journal of Farm Economics* 18, no. 2 (1936): 243.

21. Ellis W. Hawley, *The New Deal and the Problem of Monopoly: A Study in Economic Ambivalence* (Princeton: Princeton University Press, 1966), 40.

22. Meg Jacobs, *Pocketbook Politics: Economic Citizenship in Twentieth Century America* (Princeton: Princeton University Press, 2005), 96.

23. Hawley, *New Deal and the Problem of Monopoly*, 28.

24. Jacobs, *Pocketbook Politics*, 208.

25. 48 Stat. 195, 198.

26. Jacobs, *Pocketbook Politics*, 109.

27. Hawley, *New Deal and the Problem of Monopoly*, 57–62.

28. Ibid., 58, 93.

29. Ibid., 82.

30. Ibid., 96.

31. "Extension of NRA for Only 10 Months Voted By Senate," *New York Times* 5/15/1935, 1.

32. Frances Perkins, *The Roosevelt I Knew* (New York: Viking Press, 1946), 251.

Chapter 6
Countervailing Power

From the first, and increasingly through the 1930s, New Dealers asked the federal government to exercise new powers not mainly for centralized planning or social welfare, but rather, as the economist John Kenneth Galbraith would later say, "to give a group a market power it did not have before." Looking back from 1952, Galbraith noted that "the most important legislative acts of the New Deal," as well as those that "fueled the sharpest domestic controversies," were laws that enlisted the federal government in "the support of countervailing power."[1]

The idea of using the state to support private interests in the name of countervailing power attracted New Dealers for two reasons. First, it kept them on the side of American capitalism by stopping short of state ownership or even regulation of business. Second, in their understanding of history they were not the first American lawmakers to use the federal government to support private interests, they were simply the first to propose using the government mainly to benefit groups other than the owners of major corporations. As Senator Lewis Schwellenbach (D-WA) said of the nation's mythically government-free pioneer past, "Don't let anyone tell you that government bounties were not being given in those days.... The railroads got their sections of land in each township.... Vast tracts of timber lands were available for ... the timber operators.... A protective tariff system was maintained by which hidden taxes were removed from the pockets of everyone who labored in industry and agriculture. . . . There were [government] bounties galore. But the people who worked, and who bought and consumed our products never got in on them."[2]

If those policies of the nineteenth-century Republican Party succeeded in strengthening the original power within the American industrial economy—the great banks and manufacturing corporations of the Northeast—they left the rest of the country relatively underdeveloped. Not coincidentally, strong support for the New Deal came from the poorer South and West, whose voters believed they benefited little from these policies.

This historical legacy of lopsided regional riches made it happily unnecessary for the Roosevelt administration to distinguish between good politics and good policy: if they wanted to spend money to even out economic development in the country and create countervailing powers, they would spend it in the South and the West, and on the industrial workers of the country. Contrariwise, if they wanted to spend money to benefit the most loyal and critical voters in the New Deal coalition, they would spend federal money in the South and the West, and on the industrial workers of the country. Politics and economics worked together in the New Deal construction of countervailing power.

Franklin Roosevelt prided himself on inventing one way in which the government could create countervailing power, which he called the "yardstick" concept. During World War I, Roosevelt argued while assistant secretary of the navy that the U.S. government ought not to armor-plate all its own ships but rather should build a small armor-plating plant and thus learn how much the process should cost. The costs of the government-run plant would serve as a measure of fair profit for private contractors, providing a counterweight to the businessmen's information on the cost of production. The navy would then know what it ought to pay to give contractors a fair, but not excessive, profit. Roosevelt remembered this idea later.[3]

At around the time Roosevelt was urging the government to enter the armor-plating business, Washington was entering the electricity business at Muscle Shoals in Alabama. There the Tennessee River drops by 134 feet through thirty-seven miles of rapids. And there the U.S. government built Wilson Dam, providing hydroelectric power to factories producing nitrates for fertilizer or explosives.[4] Before construction on the dam had quite finished, the Harding administration proposed turning it over to private management, and the Coolidge administration in its turn supported this idea. Senator George Norris, a progressive Republican of Nebraska and chairman of the Agriculture Committee (which had charge of bills relating to fertilizer), blocked the privatization plan and instead proposed expanding public ownership of electrical production.

In the 1932 campaign Roosevelt stepped into this impasse between privatization and public ownership, saying that a few government power plants were "forever a yardstick to prevent extortion" by private monopolies. After his inauguration he worked with Norris to create the Tennessee Valley Authority (TVA), which would take over Muscle Shoals and build other dams along the river, extending government-provided power through much of the South.[5]

The law creating TVA listed among its several goals "the agricultural and industrial development of said valley."[6] Whereas a generation before, the federal government under Republican control lent itself to the development of the West by interstate private railroad corporations, under Democratic control it now pushed for the development of the South by interstate public power corporations. But interstate and public did not here mean distant or unresponsive: headquartered in Knoxville, Tennessee, TVA devoted itself to working through local institutions and

6. Civilian Conservation Corps boys weeding a Tennessee Valley Authority nursery near Wilson Dam in Alabama.

drumming up support for what its director, David Lilienthal, called "grass roots administration of federal functions." If Americans were going to adopt public ownership of electricity, Lilienthal figured, they would have to do it locally—they would never support and indeed, in the interest of democracy should never support, national socialism, contrary to the ambitions of some planners and the fears of their opponents.[7]

Democratic politicians had long yearned to raise up the South from its legacy of poverty and join it to the West as a balance to the financial and industrial (and generally Republican) centers of the Northeast and Midwest. But they had to circumvent white southerners' animosity to the federal government, whose Justice Department and civil rights policies the white South had long loathed. TVA's campaign for locally controlled federal power helped Democrats design a federal development policy white southerners could stand. Repeatedly, southern cities held referenda in which citizens voted against the private monopolies and for public power, with Lilienthal's enthusiastic support. Energetic and well-funded resistance to these votes came from private power corporations owned by the holding company of Commonwealth and Southern, which Wendell Willkie, a Democrat who supported Roosevelt in 1932, headed. TVA dampened Willkie's affection for the administration. While Willkie himself negotiated with TVA, members of Commonwealth and Southern's constituent companies fought its expansion. Southern cities and TVA responded by working to get PWA to build—or even merely to plan to build—lines and plants to compete with, and render redundant, the private power companies. Often PWA's plans alone provided enough federal leverage so the private power companies sold their infrastructure and yielded to local, public control.[8]

For much of the 1930s, Willkie's companies kept TVA from providing power to southern cities by suing and getting injunctions from courts. Although higher courts eventually ruled in TVA's favor, the long judicial process forced Lilienthal to spend months on the stump, contrasting TVA's commitment to democracy and local control to the private companies' opposition to both. Under such circumstances Lilienthal could credibly insist that though TVA's opponents might call it "soviet," it was the power companies, and not TVA, that favored the centralized, outside control of the Tennessee River Valley.

TVA illustrated typical vices and virtues of the New Deal's plans to use federal leverage to empower existing groups. It brought electrical power cheaply—at perhaps half the price Americans paid to private companies—to people who never before had it, and its success inspired private companies to try lower rates and larger markets as well. TVA also inspired Roosevelt to try rural electrification on a national scale, creating the Rural Electrification Administration in 1935 with money from the relief act of that year, to support the creation of rural power cooperatives. Like TVA, REA not only opened service to new areas, it pressed private companies to see profit potential in markets they had hitherto slighted.[9]

In these respects the effort at generating electrical power for countervailing constituencies worked, laying the foundations for further economic development in regions sorely wanting it. Inasmuch as it brought southern politicians and voters around to the New Deal, it succeeded too. At the same time, TVA's commitment to respecting local institutions limited its support for democracy: working through established southern structures meant leaving the racial hierarchy of the South intact. TVA fertilizer programs did not involve the historically black agricultural colleges of the South, nor did its segregated workforce look out of place in the land of Jim Crow.[10]

The New Deal worked to develop the West, too. Critics of the administration's motives pointed out that the swing states of the West, much more politically changeable than the Northeast or South, received a disproportionate share of the New Deal's dollars. Although PWA officials responded that more than a fair share of their budget went to the much longer settled and more developed states east of the Mississippi, it remained the case that on a per capita basis PWA money went much farther in the sparsely populated West. Likewise, if the New Deal were in the business of buying votes, western states had more electoral votes per capita to offer.

Suspicions that the Roosevelt administration was buying the West's allegiance proved weakly founded. These states had a lot of land and needed many miles of roads: if the federal government were going to spend solely on the basis of need, it would spend more money per capita on roads out West. Further, the West had plenty of projects, particularly for hydroelectric power, already planned and ready for funding. With so much land capable of sustaining so many more people, paying for these projects in the West looked like a good investment. Finally, the federal government owned disproportionate shares of land in western states—more than 80 percent of Nevada, for example—which made it cheaper and easier to build projects there.[11]

Just as spending money to develop the South made economic sense because it meant tapping the potential that slavery and its legacy had corked, spending money on the West made economic sense too: it meant making way for the denser settlement of a potentially much richer region. If New Deal development led also to environmental spoliation, if it extended the American industrial system indiscriminately, if it failed to disturb racial impediments to democracy (WPA helped intern Japanese-Americans in the West during World War II), or if it appeared suspiciously political, it also looked like a sound investment. The construction of public works under a policy of development raised up these historically underdeveloped regions as countervailing powers to the older, richer, and historically Republican Northeast. These policies also represented the most redistributive policies of the New Deal: although the Roosevelt administration may have worked to redistribute money and power geographically, it did not as directly use the state to redistribute money and power across classes.

At least since Adam Smith made *ability to pay* his first maxim of taxation, countries more comfortable with state action than the United States of the 1930s provided market power to groups that otherwise did not enjoy it by taxing people who had more wealth and using the proceeds to provide goods to people who had less. Despite the directness of this method, the New Deal did not use it. Indeed, the Roosevelt administration retained the opposite tax policy as established under Hoover in 1932, adding AAA processing taxes to regressive federal excise taxes on liquor and other goods deemed luxuries or vices. These taxes put a disproportionate burden on those Americans least able to pay. Even the Revenue Act of 1935, which resulted from Roosevelt's request for a "sound public policy of encouraging a wider distribution of wealth," touched so few people it looked like "a hell raiser, not a revenue raiser," as a member of the House Ways and Means committee claimed.[12] Believing that prospects for recovery depended on businessmen's investment, the Democrats stuck with the less-visible excise taxes—polls showed that Americans rarely considered these levies to qualify as taxes—instead of raising income taxes on more Americans.

But the Roosevelt administration did work to redistribute wealth, just not through tax policy. Instead it wanted the market to work more equitably, to allot to workers and consumers higher wages without government's direct intervention. To achieve this end the New Deal fostered the growth of worker and consumer organizations empowered to bargain collectively, and therefore more effectively, for a better deal in the marketplace. A simple theory supported this policy: if business had grown ever more organized and therefore efficient at cutting its cost, so should the buyers of products and the sellers of labor also organize and learn efficiency. In an instance of this theory's implementation, NRA promoted the organization of consumers and laborers.

Mild as toleration of a labor union's right to exist may seem, management fought it. In 1934, the country's factories exploded in strikes as corporations refused to recognize unions. Strikes shut down entire cities. Roosevelt established the National Labor Relations Board (NLRB) to settle disputes. Investigations showed the managers of American industries had determined to abort unions' birth, using infiltration, threats, speedups, and, bluntest instrument of all, the desperate job market: "Look out the window," employers said, in numerous variations in numerous workplaces, "and see the men waiting in line for your job."[13]

John L. Lewis of the United Mine Workers famously told his men, "The President wants you to join a Union."[14] Lewis exaggerated: Roosevelt disliked promoting confrontation with businessmen who would lead the country's economic recovery and viewed unions with mistrust. But as on other issues, congressmen of

Roosevelt's party pushed the president. Senator Robert Wagner drafted a bill to create a permanent NLRB and specifically to prevent the formation of company unions or the intimidation of union organizers. The law not only required companies to bargain with union representatives elected by workers but also instituted a majority rule providing that if a majority of workers in a shop voted for a union, that union would have the power to represent the whole shop.

Wagner saw the law as a way to keep from investing the state with too much power. "The National Labor Relations Board is the only key to the problem of economic stability if we intend to rely upon democratic self-help by industry and labor instead of courting the pitfalls of an arbitrary or totalitarian state."[15] Stronger unions, though a bitter pill, might go down more easily with middle-class voters than indefinitely increased federal authority and spending. And as passed by Congress in July 1935, shortly after the Supreme Court struck down the National Industrial Recovery Act, the Wagner Act replaced NRA's statist code-making authorities with the philosophy of countervailing power, attributing the economic crisis to the earlier absence of an effective counterweight to business management:

> The inequality of bargaining power between employees who do not possess full freedom of association . . . and employers who are organized in the corporate or other forms of ownership association . . . tends to aggravate recurring business depressions by depressing wage rates and reducing the purchasing power of wage earners. . . . It is hereby declared to be the policy of the United States to . . . eliminate these obstructions . . . by encouraging the practice and procedure of collective bargaining.[16]

Now the president really did want American workers to join a union—the law required it of him. And despite an unfriendly labor market (the ready availability of unemployed workers impeded unionization) Americans did join: In 1930, under a tenth of workers in manufacturing belonged to unions, while by 1940, more than a third did; in mining, the rate of unionization over the same period went from slightly over a fifth to just under three-quarters. Similar increases characterized other sectors.[17] Given the rate of unemployment, the rise in unionization as a countervailing force to managerial power owes considerably to the shift toward legal protection for unions, finally and extensively justified by the time of the Wagner Act as a way to achieve a more equitable distribution of wealth without increasing the power of the state.

Federal policy encouraged Americans to organize themselves not only as producers but also as consumers. Upon signing the National Industrial Recovery Act, Roosevelt declared, "A Consumers Advisory Board will be responsible that the interests of the consuming public will be represented" in NRA's code-making process.[18] The head of the Consumers' Advisory Board , Mary Harriman Rumsey, advertised her willingness to listen to the ordinary American consumer.[19] Complaints poured in, along with labels and other evidence of rising prices on milk, bread, and similar staples.

Similarly, AAA invited the consumers into the producers' sanctum. Frederic Howe, a municipal reformer and New York Commissioner of Immigration in the 1910s, became consumers' counsel to AAA in the summer of 1933. Howe had the job of preventing prices from rising much higher than the level necessary for producers to recover the AAA processing tax.[20] His office began producing *Consumers' Guide*, which listed prices for staple products in various American cities, showing how much over cost the prices had risen. Like Rumsey, Howe invited consumers to report price rises and especially sought discrepancies between listed and actual prices.[21]

Before long these in-house consumer voices began seeking outside help. Rumsey appointed economists and activists for the project of "building a Consumers' movement." They hoped to establish consumer councils around the country. Although the president's purported wish that Americans join labor unions did much more to organize the workforce than the consumer movement did, the New Deal's call for Americans to join consumer unions also produced a counterweight to managerial decisions and indeed to the administration's own policies. Ultimately, the consumer movement the New Deal helped build and tie to its policies lobbied to change those policies. In response to such complaints, NRA hosted a "Field Day of Criticism" that revealed widespread consumer dissatisfaction with its work. One of NRA's in-house consumer advocates, Leon Henderson, worked with economist Gardiner Means to report on the rigidity of high prices under NRA's policies, influencing Congress's reluctance to renew NRA's charter. Rising meat prices led to consumers' strikes against butchers around the country. Consumers pledged not to buy until the New Deal shifted its support from producers and processors toward buyers. One of AAA's consumer advocates, Donald Montgomery, began campaigning against rising bread prices. Having raised up the countervailing power of consumer consciousness, the New Deal responded by shifting away from its initial commitment to an alliance between government and industry, and toward a more impartial role.[22]

For these countervailing forces to have real effect they needed independence. The South and West needed development so they could generate their own wealth and capital, enabling them to represent their own regional interests against the Northeast. Workers and consumers needed organization and legitimacy so they could represent their interests independently of business management. In seeking to afford individual American workers and consumers a greater degree of independence, the Roosevelt administration determined to insure them against loss of income, either temporarily, through cyclical unemployment, or permanently, through disability or old age. To this end Roosevelt appointed a Committee on Economic Security (CES) to draft plans for social insurance.

MORE SECURITY FOR
THE AMERICAN FAMILY

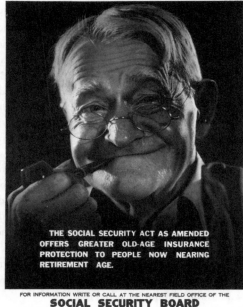

THE SOCIAL SECURITY ACT AS AMENDED
OFFERS GREATER OLD-AGE INSURANCE
PROTECTION TO PEOPLE NOW NEARING
RETIREMENT AGE.

FOR INFORMATION WRITE OR CALL AT THE NEAREST FIELD OFFICE OF THE
SOCIAL SECURITY BOARD

7. Government posters such as this promoted Social Security. Other posters promised support for widows and children of qualified workers.

The report CES sent to Roosevelt called for universal coverage of the American elderly by pensions paid for partly by their own contributions and increasingly, over time, out of the general revenues of the U.S. Treasury. Roosevelt rejected this plan, declaring it was "the same old dole under another name"—he wanted a self-financing plan under which old-age pensions worked on the model of insurance premiums. Workers and their employers would pay into a fund a percentage of their paychecks. In the event of retirement in old age, workers would draw a pension funded by their savings. The program would thus constitute "a wholly contributory scheme with the government not participating," as Roosevelt asked.[23]

Critics immediately pointed out the drawbacks of this plan. No other country financed social insurance this way, and for good reason. Contributions calculated as a percent of payroll put a relatively heavier tax burden on poorer earners. Within the administration, Harry Hopkins pointed out the regressivity of the payroll taxes and recommended a tax on wealthier Americans' incomes instead. In the press, opinion-makers fretted that "the law is almost a model of what legislation ought not to be," as the *New Republic* wrote.[24]

The administration's concern with fiscal soundness also prevented the Social Security system from reaching all Americans. Because the United States came late to the business of old-age insurance, it had the advantage of other countries' experience to examine. As Abraham Epstein, an advocate of old-age insurance, noted in 1922, "It is evident that it can only be made to apply to persons who are in regular employment. It is next to impossible to collect contributions from persons who are irregularly employed, from agricultural laborers, from those who are not their own employers, from women who work at home not for wages, from small merchants, and so forth."[25] The Roosevelt administration therefore sought to follow other countries that had excluded farm workers and domestic servants from their old-age pension policies at the start, and Congress complied.

The limits on Social Security would not last, nor did administration officials think they would. Privately, the experts knew that the contributory scheme would soon need supplementing from the general treasury. Publicly, they avowed their intention to expand the program to cover more workers when they could. As amended in 1939 and 1950, the system fulfilled these expectations. But for the moment of its creation, Social Security stuck to the limits Roosevelt set on it.

If the decisions to limit Social Security derived from a concern for fiscal soundness, they had further effects peculiar to the American workforce. The exclusion of farm workers and domestic servants disproportionately affected African Americans. At a stroke, Congress cut half the black workers in the country, and around 60 percent of those in the South, out of the Social Security system. If this racial discrimination followed from innocent concerns for fiscal stability, a further provision in the law could not so easily escape criticism.

Social Security also included a program of direct assistance to the elderly already beyond working age, who could not now contribute to funding their own pensions, setting aside federal funds to match whatever states spent to provide cash relief. It included similar plans for aid to the blind or to needy dependent children (chiefly the children of widowed mothers), on the principle that they, like the elderly, constituted a class of deserving unemployed people. The question of how much they deserved remained open.[26]

When determining how to allocate federal matching funds to the states for assistance to the elderly poor (a program distinct from the contributory insurance scheme), the Social Security proposal initially imposed on the states a uniform standard of "decency and health." Representatives of southern states protested that to meet this standard as acknowledged elsewhere in the country would require them to quadruple their aid to the poor as, indeed, the average income in the South amounted to as little as one quarter of what Americans in richer states earned. This discrepancy derived largely, as one southern senator admitted, from the different labor market imposed on the "great many colored people" in the South. Despite the obvious racist tinge to southern protestation, their provision passed with the administration's approval (and that of the sole African American in Congress, Arthur Mitchell, Democrat of Illinois, who argued it was unrealistic to expect a fourfold increase in a state's relief bill).[27]

Social Security's unemployment provisions resembled other parts of the plan: as with old-age insurance, the federal component of unemployment insurance would come from payroll taxes; as with aid to the deserving and unemployable, states would be able to determine the generosity of unemployment benefits. But unemployment compensation went further to prevent too much power from lodging in Washington. Once states established their own unemployment compensation schemes, employers could deduct what they paid their state governments from what they owed the federal government. The law thus encouraged states to establish unemployment insurance programs, rather than creating a national plan.

If, as many later commenters would claim, Social Security became the basis for the American welfare state, it did so despite its framers' apparent intentions. Its principal provisions do not qualify as welfare at all, nor as relief, owing to Roosevelt's insistence that they draw on beneficiaries' contributions rather than the general revenue. Americans did not enjoy these benefits as a matter of right, only by virtue of their having bought into the plans, as they might have with a private insurance program. Roosevelt wanted to limit federal contributions to the barest minimum in the interest of fiscal soundness—hence the contributory plan, hence the state unemployment plans, hence the matching basis for old-age assistance. "Not one nickel more.... Not one solitary nickel. Once you get off the ... matching basis the sky's the limit, and before you know it, we'll be paying the whole bill."[28]

Nor did Social Security push the United States onto a course like that followed by other modern nations, as American lawmakers chose instead a contributory system of regressive taxation. Adopting a progressive income tax for national benefits would not only have mimicked other countries' social spending and arguably have served social justice, but it might also have done a better job of fighting the Depression. But the New Dealers did not shape Social Security as a Depression-fighting policy. Rather, it constituted a guarantee of Americans' future independence from their employers and thus as an underpinning of the strategy for fostering countervailing power around the country. Moreover, it represented a modest step in that direction: reformers on the Committee on Economic Security believed that to make employees properly independent, the United States needed a system of national health insurance—but so vigorously did opponents, particularly the American Medical Association, resist even efforts to research the subject that the committee dropped it.[29] Rather than increase the power of the state, New Dealers preferred to increase the power of individual citizens and groups of citizens, and did so within what they regarded as realistic political limits.

As Franklin Roosevelt headed to reelection in 1936, he could claim to have worked both for the recovery of the American economy and for its reform, in both the interest of a fairer marketplace and the interest of the Democratic Party, which happened, owing to geographic and historical peculiarities of the American experience, to overlap. The South and the West needed economic development; the industrial Northeast needed relief from the severity of unemployment. All the great dams and roads and bridges the Roosevelt administration built, the infrastructure that brought the promise of modernity to the South and West, amounted to a minority of the New Deal's total spending, 60 percent of which went instead to relief that funneled chiefly to the more urban states of the Northeast.[30]

In responding to these needs Roosevelt was responding also to the constituents he most needed: the consumers and the workers of the industrial state and the voting citizens of the South and West, all of whom drew strength and independence from his policies. As they grew in power, they pushed the president to do more for them. In the New Deal's success lay the possibility of its demise: the louder these voices grew, the more clearly they clamored for differing goals. Roosevelt could keep them together only by extraordinary efforts and the accidents of history.

Notes

1. John Kenneth Galbraith, *American Capitalism: The Concept of Countervailing Power* (New York: Transaction Publishers, 2004), 137.

2. Jason Scott Smith, *Building New Deal Liberalism: The Political Economy of Public Works, 1933-1956* (Cambridge: Cambridge University Press, 2006), 120–21.

3. Thomas K. McCraw, *TVA and the Power Fight, 1933-1939* (Philadelphia: J. B. Lippincott Company, 1971), 30.

4. Ibid., 1.

5. Ibid., 33.

6. 48 Stat. 58.

7. David Lilienthal, *The TVA: An Experiment in The "Grass Roots" Administration of Federal Functions* (Knoxville, TN: 1939).

8. McCraw, *TVA*, 138.

9. Theodore Saloutos, *The American Farmer and the New Deal* (Ames: Iowa State University Press, 1982), 219.

10. McCraw, *TVA*, 142.

11. John Joseph Wallis, "The Political Economy of New Deal Spending Revisited, Again: With and Without Nevada," *Explorations in Economic History* 35, no. 2 (1998).

12. Mark H. Leff, *The Limits of Symbolic Reform: The New Deal and Taxation, 1933-1939* (Cambridge: Cambridge University Press, 1984), 137, 56.

13. Meg Jacobs, *Pocketbook Politics: Economic Citizenship in Twentieth Century America* (Princeton: Princeton University Press, 2005), 139.

14. Ibid., 137.

15. Ibid., 145.

16. 49 Stat. 449.

17. Irving L. Bernstein, *Turbulent Years: A History of the American Worker* (Boston: Houghton Mifflin, 1971), 769–70.

18. "President's Statement on Recovery Act Policies," *New York Times*, 6/17/1933, 2.

19. "A Champion of the Consumer Speaks Out," *New York Times*, 8/6/1933, SM5.

20. "Consumer Bureau to Check Prices," *New York Times*, 6/24/1933, 22.

21. Jacobs, *Pocketbook Politics*, 119.

22. Ibid., 131–32.

23. Mark H. Leff, "Taxing the 'Forgotten Man': The Politics of Social Security and the New Deal," *Journal of American History* 70, no. 2 (1983): 366–68.

24. Ibid.: 373.

25. Gareth Davies and Martha Derthick, "Race and Social Welfare Policy: The Social Security Act of 1935," *Political Science Quarterly* 112, no. 2 (1997): 222.

26. James T. Patterson, *America's Struggle against Poverty, 1900–1985* (Cambridge, MA: Harvard University Press, 1986), 67–75.

27. Davies and Derthick, "Race and Social Welfare Policy," 227.

28. James T. Patterson, *The New Deal and the States: Federalism in Transition* (Princeton: Princeton University Press, 1969), 93.

29. Daniel S. Hirshfield, *The Lost Reform: The Campaign for Compulsory Health Insurance in the United States from 1932 to 1943* (Cambridge, MA: Harvard University Press, 1970), 42–70.

30. Wallis, "Political Economy," 167.

Chapter 7
The End of the Beginning

Franklin Delano Roosevelt spoke with an apparently easy confidence and in the accent of an upper class indigenous to the country but normally concealed from most Americans behind the stone walls and tree-lined roads of the Hudson River Valley and Long Island. His ancestors had come to New Amsterdam in the seventeenth century, and his family never strayed far, though governments fell and rose, some abetted by Roosevelts. His mother's family, the Delanos, were merchants. He attended Groton and Harvard, schools chiefly for rich, white, Protestant boys. When he married his distant cousin Eleanor Roosevelt (making her Eleanor Roosevelt Roosevelt) he acquired as uncle-by-marriage President Theodore Roosevelt, in whose footsteps he followed as a state legislator, assistant secretary of the navy, and governor of New York. Were it not for his bout with adult polio, which left him unable to stand without much pain, effort, and assistance, he would have endured no evident hardship and, indeed, all the privilege a democratic country could offer.

Nothing in his background made him look anything like a tribune of the people; neither did he run as one in 1932, when he criticized Hoover for running deficits, nor preside as one afterward. In the United States as throughout the industrial world, the circumstances favored the growth of social spending policies, yet

Roosevelt himself, as leader of the party more favorable to such programs, resisted them. Sometimes his fiscal conservatism availed nothing, as when he opposed deposit insurance or exhibited indifference to the National Labor Relations Act until it had all but passed Congress anyway. Sometimes his conservatism permanently shaped American social policy, as when he determined the contributory and federal structure of the Social Security system. And despite his willingness to experiment, these fiscally conservative impulses never left him, which made the Roosevelt who emerged in 1936 as the champion of labor and the loudest philosopher of countervailing power all the more peculiar. When nominated for president by his party that summer, he declared war on "the privileged princes of these new economic dynasties. . . . These economic royalists complain that we seek to overthrow the institutions of America. What they really complain of is that we seek to take away their power. Our allegiance to American institutions requires the overthrow of this kind of power."[1] Roosevelt went on to "heartily subscribe" to "the brave and clear platform of this Convention," which listed "malefactors of great wealth" near "kidnappers and bandits" in the lineup of the nation's enemies.[2]

Roosevelt's opponents would sometimes call him a traitor to his class, but as the historian Richard Hofstadter observed in 1948, "if by his class one means the whole policy-making, power-wielding stratum, it would be just as true to say that his class betrayed him."[3] Despite Roosevelt's care in constructing the New Deal, despite the restraint and caution and respect for American federalism of the New Deal's every measure, despite the overriding evidence in both word and deed that the Roosevelt administration came time after time to rescue American capitalism and had no intention of replacing it, Roosevelt met at best foot-dragging, often disingenuous cooperation; as the New Deal succeeded and the Depression lessened, outright hostility from members of his class who (it turned out) regarded even slight shifts in the social order as portents of anarchy.

As much as the Democratic Party depended on the votes of segregationist whites, and as much as the Roosevelt administration built New Deal programs to respect the institutions of federalism and states' rights precisely to avoid disturbing the racial politics of the South, the New Deal nevertheless did more to assist African Americans than the Hoover administration had and more than the old Democratic Party had. The ideal of assisting the "forgotten man" compelled New Dealers with a sense of shame and history to remember that black Americans more routinely fell into that category than any other class. As First Lady, Eleanor Roosevelt ranked high among such New Dealers. She had in youth worked in a settlement house that helped the immigrant poor of New York City; she showed such sensitivity to the issues of class and race that she became the channel through which civil rights leaders like Walter White of the National Association for the Advancement of Colored People (NAACP) could make themselves heard in the

8. Ben Shahn photographed this "White Trade Only" sign—one of many around the country—in Lancaster, Ohio, for the Farm Security Administration in 1938.

White House. In particular, she pushed Hopkins at WPA to ensure that relief went to black, as well as white, workers.[4] Such efforts produced only partial success—CCC, for example, noticeably resisted racial integration—but the New Deal made inroads into black joblessness as no program, federal or state, Democratic or Republican, previously had.[5]

These changes undermined southern whites' sense of privilege, and some took this threat so seriously they decided to seek redress. One, a retired executive of the du Pont corporation, wrote another du Pont executive early in 1934 to complain, "Five negroes on my place in South Carolina refused work this spring . . . saying they had easy jobs with the government," and received the reply that perhaps some organization should appear, "for educating the people to the value of encouraging people to work; encouraging people to get rich[.]"[6] From this spark emerged the American Liberty League, which one Roosevelt aide derided as like cellophane—"first, it's a du Pont product and second, you can see right through it"—which is to say its members, despite their expressed nonpartisan concern for the U.S. Constitution, had clearly no higher goal in mind than defeating Roosevelt in 1936.[7]

A year later, the Liberty League got a valuable ally in its opposition to the New Deal: the Supreme Court of the United States. On May 27, 1935, Chief Justice Charles Evans Hughes read the majority opinion in the case of *Schechter v. United States*. The Schechter slaughterhouse owners had been convicted in federal court for selling an "unfit chicken" and other violations of the National Recovery Administration (NRA) code for the poultry industry. Hughes argued, contrary to the preamble of more than one New Deal law, "Extraordinary conditions do not create or enlarge constitutional power." The Court believed that NRA represented an unlawful delegation of power from Congress to the president and thence to the code-making authorities, and particularly that it too broadly interpreted Congress's constitutional ability to regulate interstate commerce.[8]

On May 31, Roosevelt held a press conference—"the first of its kind in White House history where a president, speaking informally ... outlined without reference to a manuscript an issue which appeared to him as second in importance only to war," as a *New York Times* reporter wrote.[9] The president read from telegrams pleading with him to restore NRA regulations, one of which suggested stripping the Supreme Court of its jurisdiction over the industrial codes. But, Roosevelt said, "these telegrams are futile." The Court's decision in *Schechter* was, he said, "more important than any decision probably since the Dred Scott case" (the case insisting the federal government had no power to prohibit slavery in the U.S. territories, which precipitated the Civil War) because the Court relied on a strict definition of the Constitution's commerce clause. Roosevelt read the decision as preventing the federal government from regulating manufacturing, mining, agriculture, and construction, even if the raw materials or finished products of those activities crossed state lines. And in a country dependent on interstate commerce, a country transformed by modern transportation and communication into a single nation, this reading of the law rendered the federal government impotent. "We have forty-eight Nations from now on.... It is a perfectly ridiculous and impossible situation," Roosevelt declared. The strict interpretation of the commerce clause might have worked when little trade crossed state lines and the nation's people moved by "horse-and-buggy." But now that "We are interdependent—we are tied together," Roosevelt said, the United States needed a national government. "Now, as to the way out ... " Roosevelt began, then stopped himself. "I suppose you will want to know something about what I am going to do. I am going to tell you very, very little on that," he said.[10]

Nor did he, for more than a year, say anything substantial in public about the Supreme Court and the New Deal, not even when the Court invalidated the Agricultural Adjustment Administration the following January and a set of other New Deal measures afterward. His opponents spoke volumes. Liberty Leaguers began lionizing the justices as defenders of the American Way. And Roosevelt's opponents began declaring that the issue of the upcoming election would be the Court. Conservative Democrat Eugene Talmadge of Georgia asked whether America's voters wanted "a bunch of Communists . . . to appoint the successors" to the aging justices. Republicans said Roosevelt had gone beyond the conventions of American civility with his "horse-and-buggy" comments, and their nominee, Governor Alf Landon of Kansas, said that Roosevelt had "cracked up."[11] Senator Arthur Vandenberg (R-MI), disingenuously ruminated, "I don't think the President has any thought of emulating Mussolini, Hitler or Stalin, but his utterance as I have heard it is exactly what these men would say."[12]

Although Roosevelt said little, his administration and Congress kept active, passing the Wagner Act to re-create and strengthen labor's right to organize as recognized in the National Industrial Recovery Act, and passing the Guffey Coal Act to create a miniature NRA specifically for the bituminous coal industry, on the grounds that this industry operated on a truly interstate scope.[13]

The Court kept pace with the New Dealers, invalidating the Coal Act in May 1936, as one of a string of decisions that over the course of a year pitted its majorities against the New Deal in opinions that struck Felix Frankfurter, then a law professor at Harvard, as "written for morons" and left him fuming, "Apparently history and precedents mean nothing."[14] Nor were Harvard faculty the only Americans appalled. The president reliably received letters from constituents complaining, as one Texas man did, that "I told you the Rich Men always Run to the Supreme Court to Beat Our Laws."[15]

Ultimately the Court outstripped the federal legislators and ran ahead to put a roadblock in front of the states. In *Morehead v. New York ex. rel. Tipaldo*, the Court ruled that states could not set minimum wages for women workers. Roosevelt mildly commented, "It seems to be fairly clear … that the 'no-man's-land' where no Government—State or Federal—can function is being more clearly defined. A State cannot do it and the Federal Government cannot do it."[16] Some Republicans recognized that with this decision, defending the Supreme Court no longer looked like such a fine election strategy. Congressman Hamilton Fish (R-NY) said, "I say to my Republican friends if you lend or express any sympathy for this decision … it will mean a million votes for the Democratic party." Herbert Hoover remarked, "something should be done to give back to the states the powers they thought they already had."[17]

But by now the Republicans had so thoroughly committed themselves to a policy of standing with the Court against Roosevelt they could not easily reverse course. At the Republican National Convention, Hoover insisted, "The American should thank Almighty God for the Constitution and the Supreme Court," and got two minutes' applause.[18] In the *New York Times*, Arthur Krock wrote, "the court knows itself to be on trial."[19] If so, the Court had put itself in the dock, and the Republicans had climbed in with it—Roosevelt, in his near-total silence on judicial issues, had little to do with it. The election amounted to a referendum on the Court only inasmuch as it ranked much more importantly as a referendum on the New Deal, and not the New Deal as a particular program or even a success but as a willingness to use the power of the U.S. government on behalf of working and suffering Americans. While his opponents stood by the Supreme Court and against the New Deal, Roosevelt stood by the New Deal and against the Depression. In Madison Square Garden on October 31, he said, "Tonight I call the roll—the roll of honor of those who stood with us in 1932 and still stand with us today. Written on it are the names of millions who never had a chance—men at starvation wages, women in sweatshops, children at looms." And arrayed against them

the old enemies of peace—business and financial monopoly, speculation, reckless banking, class antagonism, sectionalism, war profiteering. They had begun to consider the Government of the United States as a mere appendage to their own affairs. . . . They are unanimous in their hate for me—and I welcome their hatred. I should like to have it said of my first Administration that in it the forces of selfishness and of lust for power met their match. I should like to have it said of my second Administration that in it these forces met their master.[20]

The electorate assented. All the states but Maine and Vermont went for Roosevelt. No president had enjoyed such a majority in the electoral college since James Monroe ran virtually unopposed in 1820, and Roosevelt won a larger share of the popular vote (more than 60 percent) than any other candidate since careful record-keeping began in 1824.[21] Roosevelt won unprecedented majorities of African American and Jewish voters. But most importantly he drew working people to the polls in record numbers to vote for the president they knew stood by them. Pollsters found that middle-class people were more likely to vote for the president than the rich, and the working class were more likely to vote for the president than the middle class. Even within the working class, this gradation showed itself: going down the scale of skills, the less-skilled workers were more likely to support the president than the more-skilled ones. The American people had a good idea where their president stood. As one wrote him, "you are the one & only President that ever helped a Working Class of People."[22] At the same time, the voices in the land that had sought to challenge Roosevelt for leadership of the middle and working classes had fallen silent. Huey Long had been murdered the year before. Father Charles Coughlin, the radio priest, led an unsuccessful third party effort, earned rebuke from the Catholic Church for his politics, and lost listeners as he became increasingly anti-Semitic. Even the Communist Party in the United States avoided criticizing Roosevelt.[23]

The astounding national majority that Roosevelt had built would last for about thirty years, but even at the moment of its triumph the fissures that would crack it apart had already opened. A coalition whose political program as a matter of principle used the federal government to aid working-class, ethnic, and African Americans was a coalition that appealed almost entirely to urban Americans. This coalition might well succeed in electing a president, as populous cities could carry populous states with many electoral votes. But the structure of Congress and especially of the Senate resisted this politics of class and city, largely because the eighteenth-century framers meant the Congress to do just that. Rural areas, areas with smaller towns, and the white South with its persistent racist politics looked with increasing hostility on the Roosevelt administration as the president—with increasing frankness—declared himself the champion of the country's downtrodden. Roosevelt won reelection on a newly clear New Deal, but he also laid bare the difference between the New Deal and the Democratic Party.[24]

Roosevelt spent the first year of his second term clarifying this difference in a manner he would not have chosen, with his first major political loss. Despite the president's own silence about the Supreme Court in 1936, advocates of judicial reform spoke often about changing the Court's composition, recalling the Reconstruction era when a Republican Congress had stripped the Court of jurisdiction in some cases and shifted its numbers. One of the president's advisors discovered that the New Deal's great foe on the Court, Justice James McReynolds, when serving as Woodrow Wilson's attorney general in 1913, had proposed to reform the federal judiciary by requiring the appointment of a new judge for each judge who did not retire on his seventieth birthday. The Supreme Court's four most anti-New Deal justices were all over seventy, and none of the justices was under sixty. Roosevelt settled on McReynolds's plan for increasing the Court's numbers—or as supporters privately and opponents publicly said, "packing" the Court.[25]

Well before the president committed himself to the plan, the Court apparently reacted. In December, after the election but before the inauguration, Justice Owen Roberts, who had previously voted with four other anti-New Deal justices to make a majority on the Court, switched his vote to a new, pro-New Deal majority in a case that looked to almost all observers like a frank reversal. The Court would not read its opinion in *West Coast Hotel v. Parrish* until March, but in it the justices said the opposite of what they had said in *Tipaldo*—that the states could indeed legislate minimum wages.[26] And soon they would uphold the Wagner Act and the Social Security Act, and afterward seemed much friendlier to the New Deal in all its respects.

Yet Roosevelt went ahead with his plan to shift the Court. Supporters could claim the idea had obvious merits: the Republicans packed the Court during Reconstruction; Theodore Roosevelt advocated similar measures during and after his presidency; when Franklin Roosevelt entered office fewer than 30 percent of federal judges were Democrats and through his entire first term he had not been able to appoint a Supreme Court justice; *Tipaldo* in particular struck almost everyone as obviously at odds with the times and tradition.[27] But the Court-packing plan presented an excellent opportunity to level at Roosevelt the charge of dictatorial ambition which, in an unsettled age of actual dictators in developed countries, carried special weight. The Senate Judiciary Committee issued a report repudiating the president's plan as a "needless, futile, and utterly dangerous abandonment of constitutional principle" that reminded them of the misfortunes other countries' political systems had recently suffered. Seven of the ten signers were Democrats. As one journalist wrote, the report looked like conservative Democrats' "document of secession."[28]

As the summer went on, and the Court looked ever more conciliatory, Roosevelt's Court-packing plan looked increasingly unnecessary. It finally went down to defeat amid death—Senator Joseph T. Robinson (D-AR), Roosevelt's floor leader, died while pressing the bill—and death threats from vigilante opponents of the president, and the administration's congressional support faded away.[29]

The protracted Court fight and the split within the Democratic Party worked with a larger hardship to undermine the New Deal. For the first time since Roosevelt's election and with sickening speed, the country plunged into economic recession, imperiling the New Deal's claims to success. It did not look like an ordinary reversal of the business cycle, as the economy had clearly not completely recovered from the fall of 1929. Administration critics blamed the recession on Roosevelt. They said he had scared businessmen into holding onto their capital, thus preventing them from making productive investments, and they also blamed the Social Security taxes, which had gone into effect in 1937, for removing money from the economy. Within the administration, New Dealers blamed businessmen for deliberately refusing to invest—for starting what they called a "capital strike," to discredit the New Deal—and they too blamed Roosevelt: in a resurgence of his fiscal conservatism, Roosevelt had ordered cuts in public works spending with the goal of balancing the budget.[30] As New Deal spending fell, unemployment rose.[31]

In a private letter to the president dated February 1, 1938, John Maynard Keynes argued that Roosevelt ought to act as if all critics were right. Cutting relief spending was, Keynes said, "an error of optimism," and renewed spending on public works would help reverse the downturn. At the same time, Keynes noted, the United States needed private enterprise to help solve its problems: "You could do anything you liked with them, if you would treat them (even the big ones), not as wolves and tigers, but as domestic animals by nature, even though they have been badly brought up and not trained as you would wish.... If you work them into the surly, obstinate, terrified mood, of which domestic animals, wrongly handled, are so capable, the nation's burdens will not get carried to market." So Roosevelt needed to reenlist businessmen in the recovery effort. Keynes's recommendations carried extra weight now, as he had in 1936 published *The General Theory of Employment, Money, and Interest*, which together with the recession encouraged American economists to believe that a government's deficit spending could bring about a recovery from recession by getting consumers to buy more.[32]

Roosevelt acted as if he believed at least half of Keynes's argument. In the spring of 1938, Roosevelt asked for a resumption of public works spending, admitting that it "began to taper off too quickly" in 1937.[33] In June, Congress obliged, making about $3 billion available for renewed relief spending and dramatically raising federal contributions to the economy.[34] But by this time the Court fight and the recession had weakened Roosevelt. Apart from the increase of relief spending, he got from Congress the Fair Labor Standards Act, which banned child labor and set a federal minimum wage.[35] But Roosevelt won that law only with considerable help from a long campaign waged by the National Consumers' League and some major labor unions.[36] Afterward the New Dealers could no longer produce significant new law.

The president now attacked two major sources of opposition. Against organized business, Roosevelt arrayed the Temporary National Economic Committee (TNEC), which aimed to expose the bad practices of monopolists. And against conservative southern Democrats he launched a personal campaign. Both efforts failed. TNEC conducted hearings into various industries and considered a variety of methods to end, or at least to regulate, monopolies. While it discovered and duly reported reams of data on American industry, it came up with no clear proposal for action against the trusts and holding companies that controlled American businesses. But it did emphasize that government must play the role Keynes prescribed, of promoting prosperity by spending gauged to encourage consumer purchasing.[37]

Roosevelt himself took a more traditionally partisan approach to the economy, identifying the South as "the Nation's No. 1 economic problem," and targeting it as the Democratic Party's number one political problem: "I think the South is going to remain Democratic, but I think it is going to be a more intelligent form of democracy than has kept the South for other reasons, in the Democratic column for all these years. . . . it is going to be a liberal democracy."[38] Roosevelt campaigned without success against sitting southern Democrats through the summer of 1938, and they reacted by invoking the specter that had stirred white southern hearts since the Civil War: outside interference by Yankee agitators. In the November congressional elections, the American electorate registered general disillusionment with the president, returning a House of Representatives in which the Democratic delegation lost seventy-two seats and a Senate in which the Democratic delegation lost seven seats.[39] Roosevelt's prediction proved incorrect. The South would not turn liberal, nor even remain Democratic if the Democrats insisted on trying to change its race relations: in ten years' time, his successor, Harry S Truman, would narrowly avoid defeat when the South bolted the Democratic Party because it adopted the cause of civil rights for African Americans.

From the high of 1936 to the low of 1938, Roosevelt demonstrated what the New Deal could and could not do to American politics. On a national level at the polls in a presidential election, the president could successfully present himself as the champion of the people and their New Deal against an old guard of the rich and hidebound. He could ride the rhetoric and the reality of class politics to reelection. But American laws and customs do not provide for the national organization of politics. And against a Congress elected from localities, against a Senate elected from states, Roosevelt's cross-sectional politics foundered. In 1938 the president's mailbag clearly showed the divisions between sections of the country. While some wrote with praise and to ask, as one woman did, "How can anybody be against you?! You have kept so many parents and children together through W.P.A.," others clearly were against him. One woman said, "It makes me sick at heart, to think you have nothing on your program only the same old thing you have had for 5 yrs. just giving to those who will take it," and one man asked, "Did it ever enter your head that the country ran before your time and will after your gone?"[40]

It is also fair to say that apart from health insurance, Roosevelt and Congress between them set in place American versions of the major components of social security as it existed in other industrial countries, including provision for the elderly, the unemployed, the disabled, and the otherwise dependent. They shored up the banks and the currency and, by their lights, saved American capitalism. They launched the development of underdeveloped regions in the South and the West. True, some goals failed, like the extension of the TVA model to other regions.[41] And already the Democrats had discovered the political peril that awaited them when they edged even a little bit toward the specifically American necessity of civil rights for black citizens.

Late in the 1930s, policymakers who had come to Washington to change the way the nation worked found themselves increasingly asked to find ways to make the existing structure of the American economy work a bit better. Agencies like the National Resources Planning Board discounted the idea of structural changes in favor of using government to improve existing institutions.[42] Congress patched up programs, re-creating AAA to keep parity policies in place without offending the Supreme Court and amending Social Security. New Dealers increasingly accepted the policy generally described as Keynesianism—that through the federal budget they could promote Americans' spending and thus overall economic growth without meddling in the basic workings or balance of the economy.

But though at the legislative level the creative phase of the New Deal was ending, as an idea distilled from those legislative conflicts and compromises it had only just begun its life. The idea was a simple one, as a WPA relief worker said in 1938:

The way I look at it is this. This is a rich country. I figger it ain't going to hurt the government to feed and clothe them that needs it. Half of 'em can't get work, or just ain't fixed to handle work if they get it.... We've got the money. Plenty of it. No sense in the big fellows kicking about a little handout to the poor. Matter's not if some ain't deserving.... Lot of 'em that comes here, why I'd sooner give them a kick in the pants than shove 'em out supplies. But you got to take the good with the bad. Or bad with the good, whichever way you've a mind to put it.[43]

The idea in this speech, the idea that it did a rich country no harm to help even the unworthy poor came out of the New Deal; and so indeed did the speech itself and so also did the idea that a rich country ought to record and keep it, plain utterance of an ordinary person though it was.

The speech remains because WPA preserved it, along with the musings of many other Americans. The Federal Writers' Project of WPA, together with a number of other similar projects, sent writers around the country to record Americans—not just their opinions of the New Deal, or the Depression, or the president, but anything and everything, their lives and hopes and ambitions and idle irritations, not to ennoble the New Deal or the nation but simply to give the culture a record of itself and its people. The writers worked as carefully as they could, following instructions to "take down the exact words of the informant."[44] They recorded how Americans spoke, sang, worked, and played. Their colleagues with cameras recorded how the people and the country looked. They interviewed current sharecroppers and former slaves: "I lays in the bunk two days, getting over that whipping, gitting over it in the body but not the heart. No sir, I has that in the heart to this day."[45] They found onetime pioneer settlers, and Indians who remembered when the pioneer settlers came. They wrote down tall tales, ghost stories, and folk songs, the stuff of the country's rural past now vanishing in the newly national, urban nation. And they published it, in *The Jewish Landsmanschaften of New York*

(1938), *U.S. One: Maine to Florida* (1938), *The Negro in Virginia* (1940), *The Havasupai and the Hualapai* (1940), among dozens of other books on every state and people and feature of the landscape.

With the Federal Art Project and the Federal Theatre Project, WPA also made new culture for the country. The art project made murals and posters with a distinctive visual style. And the theater project ensured that Americans could see plays like *Macbeth* or *Dr. Faustus*, *The Mikado* or an adaptation of Sinclair Lewis's novel warning about the potential for fascism in America, *It Can't Happen Here*, not only in New York but in cities around the country.

These cultural ambitions of the New Deal came to grief on the same opposition as its political ambitions. Conservative, particularly southern, Democrats like Congressman Martin Dies of Texas, began fretting publicly about Communist influence on the New Deal. Dies's Un-American Activities Committee began hearings in 1938 to investigate the influence of Communism on unions and the New Deal broadly, including the Federal Theatre Project. In December, Hallie Flanagan, the Project's director, went before the committee. When she mentioned Christopher Marlowe, who wrote *Dr. Faustus*, Congressman Joseph Starnes asked her, "You are quoting from this Marlowe. Is he a Communist?" Flanagan replied, "Put in the record...that he was the greatest dramatist in the period of Shakespeare, immediately preceding Shakespeare."[46] The exchange illustrated the breadth of the gap between the culture the New Dealers were promulgating and the culture in some regions of the country asked to appreciate it. By 1939 the Dies Committee had helped end funding for the Federal Theatre Project, and the conservatives in Congress turned their attention to other New Deal agencies. In the summer of 1939 they began looking into NLRB, and conservative Democrats and Republicans voted together to defeat spending bills Roosevelt had proposed.[47]

9. Poster for the Federal Theatre Project staging of Sinclair Lewis's *It Can't Happen Here.*

As conservative opposition stymied him, Roosevelt began thinking past the New Deal. One of his advisors said that in 1940 the president told him, "he has probably gone as far as he can on domestic questions." The war in Europe began to claim his attention. And though he would tell the remaining New Dealers "we must start winning the war," he did not quite abandon the New Deal, even as the nation began to fight.[48]

10. This WPA Federal Art Project mural in San Francisco's George Washington High School depicts a scene from the American Revolution.

Notes

1. Franklin D. Roosevelt, "Acceptance Speech for the Renomination for the Presidency," June 27, 1936, Philadelphia, PA. Checked online, 2/27/2007, at www.presidency.ucsb.edu/shownomination.php?convid=37.

2. James MacGregor Burns, *Roosevelt: The Lion and the Fox* (New York: Harcourt, Brace and Company, 1956), 272.

3. Richard Hofstadter, *The American Political Tradition and the Men Who Made It* (New York: Vintage, 1989), 435.

4. Harvard Sitkoff, *A New Deal for Blacks* (New York: Oxford University Press, 1978), 60.

5. Bruce J. Schulman, *From Cotton Belt to Sunbelt: Federal Policy, Economic Development, and the Transformation of the South, 1938–1980* (Durham, NC: Duke University Press, 1994), 34.

6. Frederick Rudolph, "The American Liberty League, 1934–1940," *The American Historical Review* 56, no. 1 (1950): 19.

7. William E. Leuchtenburg, *The FDR Years: On Roosevelt and His Legacy* (New York: Columbia University Press, 1995), 124.

8. 295 U.S. 495, 528.

9. Charles W. Hurd, "President Says End of NRA Puts Control Up to People," *New York Times* 6/1/1935, 1.

10. Franklin D. Roosevelt, press conference, May 31, 1935. Checked online, 3/1/2007, www.presidency.ucsb.edu/ws/print.php?pid=15065.

11. William E. Leuchtenburg, "When the People Spoke, What Did They Say?: The Election of 1936 and the Ackerman Thesis," *Yale Law Journal* 108, no. 8 (1999): 2088, 2080.

12. Leuchtenburg, "The Origins of Franklin D. Roosevelt's 'Court-Packing' Plan," *Supreme Court Review* 1966 (1966): 358.

13. 49 Stat. 991; "The Bituminous Coal Conservation Act of 1935," *Yale Law Journal* 45, no. 2 (1935).

14. Leuchtenburg, "When the People Spoke," 2106; Leuchtenburg, "Comment on Laura Kalman's Article, 'The Constitution, the Supreme Court, and the New Deal'," *American Historical Review* 110, no. 4 (2005).

15. Leuchtenburg, "The Origins of Franklin D. Roosevelt's 'Court-Packing' Plan," 355.

16. Leuchtenberg, "When the People Spoke," 2084.

17. Ibid., 2090.

18. Ibid.

19. Arthur Krock, "In Washington," *New York Times* 5/27/1936, 22.

20. Franklin D. Roosevelt, "Address at Madison Square Garden, New York City," 10/31/1936. Checked online 3/7/2007 at www.presidency.ucsb.edu/ws/print.php?pid=15219.

21. Leuchtenburg, *FDR Years*, 145–46.

22. Ibid., 153.

23. Alan Brinkley, *The End of Reform: New Deal Liberalism in Recession and War* (New York: Vintage, 1995), 257–62, Leuchtenburg, *FDR Years*, 137.

24. James T. Patterson, *Congressional Conservatism and the New Deal: The Growth of the Conservative Coalition in Congress, 1933–1939* (Westport, CT: Greenwood Press, 1981).

25. Leuchtenburg, "The Origins of Franklin D. Roosevelt's 'Court-Packing' Plan," 390–99.

26. Leuchtenburg , "Comment on Laura Kalman's Article."

27. Leuchtenburg, "The Origins of Franklin D. Roosevelt's 'Court-Packing' Plan," 349, n. 8.

28. Leuchtenburg, "FDR's Court-Packing Plan: A Second Life, a Second Death," *Duke Law Journal* 1985, no. 3/4 (1985): 675–77.

29. Ibid.: 685–87.

30. "President Plans 600,000 WPA Cut," *New York Times*, 1/26/1937, 2.

31. Patrick Renshaw, "Was There a Keynesian Economy in the USA between 1933 and 1945?," *Journal of Contemporary History* 34, no. 3 (1999): 343–44.

32. William J. Barber, *Designs within Disorder: Franklin D. Roosevelt, the Economists, and the Shaping of American Economic Policy, 1933–1945* (Cambridge: Cambridge University Press, 1996), 108–12; Brinkley, *End of Reform*, 82–85, 94–97.

33. Lester V. Chandler, *American Monetary Policy, 1928–41* (New York: Harper and Row, 1971), 325–26.

34. 52 Stat. 809 and E. Cary Brown, "Fiscal Policy in the 'Thirties: A Reappraisal," *American Economic Review* 46, no. 5 (1956); Chandler, *American Monetary Policy*, 254.

35. 52 Stat. 1060.

36. Landon R. Y. Storrs, *Civilizing Capitalism: The National Consumers' League, Women's Activism, and Labor Standards in the New Deal Era* (Chapel Hill: University of North Carolina Press, 2000), 177–205.

37. Brinkley, *End of Reform*, 122–31.

38. Schulman, *From Cotton Belt*, 49–50.

39. Checked on the Clerk of the House website, 3/8/2007, http:// clerk.house.gov/art_history/house_history/partyDiv.html, and the Senate Historian website, 3/8/2007, www.senate.gov/pagelayout/ history/one_item_and_teasers/partydiv.htm.

40. Lawrence W. Levine and Cornelia R. Levine, eds., *The People and the President: America's Conversation with FDR* (Boston: Beacon Press, 2002), 234–35, 241.

41. Leuchtenburg, "Roosevelt, Norris and the 'Seven Little TVAs,' " *Journal of Politics* 14, no. 3 (1952).

42. Patrick D. Reagan, *Designing a New America: The Origins of New Deal Planning, 1890–1943* (Amherst: University of Massachusetts Press, 1999); Brinkley, *End of Reform*, 245–61.

43. [Federal Writers' Project], *These Are Our Lives* (New York: W. W. Norton, 1975), 366.

44. Joint Committee on Folk Arts, WPA folksong questionnaire, 1939. Library of Congress Digital ID AFCTS wpa001, viewed online 3/8/07.

45. Jerre Mangione, *The Dream and the Deal: The Federal Writers' Project, 1935–1943* (New York: Avon, 1972), 264.

46. Roy Rosenzweig and Barbara Melosh, "Government and the Arts: Voices from the New Deal Era," *Journal of American History* 77, no. 2 (1990): 596.

47. Patterson, *Congressional Conservatism*, 321–22.

48. Brinkley, *End of Reform*, 144.

Conclusion

The New American Way at Home and Around the World

In November 1938, just months after the Fair Labor Standards Act passed, Roosevelt privately told his secretary of the treasury, Henry Morgenthau, that the world's slide into war might well benefit Americans generally and the Democrats politically. "These foreign orders" for armaments, Roosevelt said, "mean prosperity in this country and we can't elect a Democratic Party unless we get prosperity." At the same time Roosevelt began thinking about building up American military power as a deterrent, to avoid having to negotiate with Hitler.[1] Despite losses in the 1938 congressional elections, the Democratic Party remained in power, as did Roosevelt for an unprecedented third term in 1940. And in a few years he told reporters he "no longer like[d] the term 'New Deal'," that "Dr. New Deal" had come to save the country from one set of ills, but now that it faced new perils, "his partner . . . Dr. Win-the-War," would take over.[2]

Roosevelt's substitution of "win-the-war" for "New Deal" mirrored shifts in the federal budget. Congress ended the New Deal, even as war allowed the government to spend the public's money with a zeal and abandon that mere global economic crisis could not support. By the end of 1943, Congress had abolished CCC, WPA, and other New Deal agencies.[3] At the same time, federal spending grew from 8 percent of US GDP in 1938 to 40 percent in 1943.[4] The war let federal officials hire Americans directly without a second thought as to whether they were instituting anything so un-American as national work-relief. War spending and employment dwarfed Depression spending and employment, and in 1943, at long last, unemployment (measured as a percentage of the civilian labor force) dropped below its 1929 level.[5] As the economist E. Cary Brown noted in 1956, the New Deal never seriously tested Keynes's recommendations: "[f]iscal policy, then, seems to have been an unsuccessful recovery device in the 'thirties—not because it did not work, but because it was not tried."[6] Only the war brought that trial, and then not as an experiment in recovery, but as an incident of military necessity.

Yet the war did not wholly displace the idea of the New Deal, and when Roosevelt began to consider what lay beyond the fighting, he resorted to the ideals of the 1930s. In January 1944, Roosevelt delivered his State of the Union address, declaring, "It is our duty now to begin to lay the plans and determine the strategy for the winning of a lasting peace. . . . We have come to a clear realization of the fact that true individual freedom cannot exist without economic security and independence." He then went on to list, "a second Bill of Rights under which a new basis of security and prosperity can be established for all regardless of station, race, or creed." The new rights included

> The right to a useful and remunerative job in the industries or shops or farms or mines of the Nation;
>
> The right to earn enough to provide adequate food and clothing and recreation;
>
> The right of every farmer to raise and sell his products at a return which will give him and his family a decent living;
>
> The right of every businessman, large and small, to trade in an atmosphere of freedom from unfair competition and domination by monopolies at home or abroad;
>
> The right of every family to a decent home;

The right to adequate medical care and the opportunity to achieve
and enjoy good health;

The right to adequate protection from the economic fears of old
age, sickness, accident, and unemployment;

The right to a good education.

Roosevelt concluded, "All of these rights spell security. And after
this war is won we must be prepared to move forward, in the
implementation of these rights, to new goals of human happiness
and well-being."[7]

Time magazine remarked that "Dr. Win-the-War has apparently
called into consultation Dr. Win-New-Rights."[8] But many of the
rights—to security from economic hardship, to employment, to
good farm prices, to vigorous business commerce, to a living wage
and a home—already had New Deal programs designed to ensure
their implementation. And others—to medical care and to
education—developed easily from New Deal principles. They
found fuller expression in Roosevelt's plans for the peace, not only
for America, but for the world.[9]

As the New Deal wound down its ambitious domestic program,
the Roosevelt administration began looking outward again.
Secretary of State Cordell Hull, like Keynes, had for decades
believed that an open world economy would tend toward peace
and prosperity. "[U]nhampered trade," Hull said, "dovetailed with
peace."[10] To this end he worked to secure trade agreements
including the Anglo-American Trade Agreement of 1938, which
contributed to the idea that international cooperation might
restore the global economy of the era before World War I.

Near the end of World War II, ideas like Hull's approached fruition.
In June 1944, John Maynard Keynes went to the United States to
represent Britain at the Bretton Woods conference. On paper
Keynes rated as only one of 730 delegates from forty-four countries

convening to establish rules for the postwar economy. But in person Keynes played the role of protagonist at the conference. In 1941, before the United States had entered the war, he had drafted a plan to supply part of what the Versailles Treaty left out—a system to ensure the smooth operation of the world's finance and commerce, to "prevent the piling up of credit and debit balances without limit"—after all, the cardinal rule for the postwar economy would be to avoid reproducing the prewar economy.[11] Keynes's plan for an International Clearing Union would allot governments credit based on their share of world trade and allow them to draw that credit, denominated in a notional banking currency, the Bancor, as needed to keep their economies stable.

Morally alongside Keynes stood his antagonist, the American representative Harry Dexter White. White had his own plan to solve the same problem by slightly different solutions: governments would still borrow, but from a contributory fund rather than from a pool of Bancors.[12] White's plan stood in much the same relation to Keynes's idea as the New Deal stood in relation to European welfare states. Under British programs to address poverty and disability, as drawn up in the Beveridge plan of 1942, citizens received benefits from the state as a matter of right. Nobody got pensions as a matter of right under Social Security—retirees drew benefits because they had contributed.

The American delegation rejected Keynes's plan and insisted on White's for much the same reason the Roosevelt administration had insisted on a contributory basis for Social Security: a contributory scheme would limit claims and satisfy Congress. Thus White's plan became the major basis for the International Monetary Fund (IMF) as agreed at Bretton Woods, and Congress placed further restrictions on IMF to prevent unconditional withdrawals from the fund.[13]

IMF had a twin, the International Bank for Reconstruction and Development, better known as the World Bank. Where IMF was supposed to allow countries to weather the vicissitudes of free economies, the World Bank was supposed to lend money for the repair of war damage and for long-poor countries to enter the club of modern nations. It stood in relation to the world's less-developed regions rather as PWA, TVA, and WPA stood to the American South and West. Also rather like those New Deal relief agencies, the World Bank labored under the limits of prevailing economic opinion, which limited also the bank's capital: its first loan to France committed a full third of its available resources.[14]

Even more like the New Deal's domestic programs, the limited resources of IMF and the World Bank provided the basis for experimentation, for discarding failure and building upon success, surviving even Roosevelt's death in April 1945. Just as with the early New Deal, constraints on the early Bretton Woods system failed to produce global economic recovery: the World Bank could not supply enough money for reconstruction, and IMF refused to lend money unless assured it would be used only to correct short-term imbalances, not for reconstruction at all.[15] And just as in the New Deal, innovative U.S. policymakers established a new program to meet the need: in 1947 a State Department official wrote, "Communist movements are threatening established governments in every part of the globe. These movements feed on economic and political weakness. The countries under Communist pressure require economic assistance on a large scale if they are to maintain their territorial integrity and political independence. At one time it had been expected that the International Bank [for Reconstruction and Development, i.e., the World Bank] could satisfy the needs for such assistance. But it is now clear that the Bank cannot do this job.... The only way to meet this challenge is by a vast new programme of assistance given directly by the United States itself."[16]

This conviction became the basis for the European Recovery Program, better known as the Marshall Plan, after Secretary of State

George Marshall, who declared, "The United States should do whatever it is able to do to assist in . . . the revival of a working economy in the world so as to permit the emergence of political and social conditions in which free institutions can exist." Shortly afterward, IMF liberalized its lending policy, and the U.S. dollar, still tied to gold at $35 per ounce, became the base currency of a revamped Bretton Woods system that lasted for about twenty-five years.[17]

By 1947, thirty years after it entered World War I, the U.S. government had come around to something approaching Keynes's view after Versailles—that as the world's richest country it had an obligation to restore the world's economy to health. The American leadership reached this conclusion hesitantly and only when prodded by crisis: they preferred much more modest experimentation than the brilliant Keynes prescribed. The halting, piecemeal efforts of the New Deal and then of the Bretton Woods system solved problems slowly and partially, and thus let the United States and the world drift rather closer to disaster than a simple Keynesian move might have done. But the programs met with ultimate success: Bretton Woods fostered greater economic stability and more rapid economic growth than eras before or since.[18]

The openly experimental, obviously fallible, always compromised quality of the New Deal programs and their progeny reflected the imperfect democracy that gave them birth. Considering the costs of this painful process, we might prefer a program of comprehensive change to Roosevelt's caution. But weighing also the performance of his administration's jerry-built machinery both at home and abroad against the record of more sweeping, ideologically and theoretically coherent programs (including those that attacked the New Deal), we might better appreciate the merits of the Roosevelt era's limits. The New Deal's evident imperfection invited criticism and further tinkering, making way for improvements to the American democracy in the years afterward and yet to come.

Notes

1. Michael S. Sherry, *The Rise of American Air Power: The Creation of Armageddon* (New Haven: Yale University Press, 1987), 81.
2. "The Nine Hundred and Twenty-Ninth Press Conference," *The Public Papers and Addresses of Franklin D. Roosevelt*, ed. Samuel I. Rosenman, 1943, vol., 571.
3. Alan Brinkley, *The End of Reform: New Deal Liberalism in Recession and War* (New York: Vintage, 1995), 141.
4. Susan B. Carter et al., eds., *Historical Statistics of the United States, Earliest Times to the Present, Millennial Edition* (New York: Cambridge University Press, 2006), series Ea636 and Ca10.
5. Ibid., series Ba475. Unemployment was 2.89 percent in 1929 and 1.77 percent in 1943.
6. E. Cary Brown, "Fiscal Policy in the 'Thirties: A Reappraisal," *The American Economic Review* 46, no. 5 (1956): 863–66.
7. "President Roosevelt's Message to Congress," *New York Times* 1/12/1944, 12.
8. Cited in Cass R. Sunstein, *The Second Bill of Rights: FDR's Unfinished Revolution and Why We Need It More Than Ever* (New York: Basic Books, 2004), 15.
9. On the question of Roosevelt's sincerity in this speech, see James T. Kloppenberg, "Franklin Delano Roosevelt, Visionary," *Reviews in American History* 34, no. 4 (2006).
10. Quoted in Arthur W. Schatz, "The Anglo-American Trade Agreement and Cordell Hull's Search for Peace 1936–1938," *Journal of American History* 57, no. 1 (1970).
11. Cited in Elizabeth Borgwardt, *A New Deal for the World: America's Vision for Human Rights* (Cambridge, MA: Belknap Press of Harvard University Press, 2005), 108.
12. See Ibid., 109.
13. Richard N. Gardner, *Sterling-Dollar Diplomacy in Current Perspective: The Origins and Prospects of Our International Economic Order*, New, exp. ed. (New York: Columbia University Press, 1980), 134–36.
14. Edward S. Mason and Robert E. Asher, *The World Bank since Bretton Woods* (Washington, DC: The Brookings Institution, 1973), 105.
15. Gardner, *Sterling-Dollar*, 297.
16. Ibid., 300.

17. Gardner, *Sterling-Dollar*, 302.
18. Barry Eichengreen, "Epilogue: Three Perspectives on the Bretton Woods System," in *A Retrospective on the Bretton Woods System: Lessons for International Monetary Reform*, ed. Michael D. Bordo and Barry Eichengreen (Chicago: University of Chicago Press, 1993), 626.

Further Reading

Badger, Anthony J. *The New Deal: The Depression Years, 1933–40*. London: Macmillan, 1989.

Berlin, Isaiah. "President Franklin Delano Roosevelt." In *The Proper Study of Mankind: An Anthology of Essays*, edited by Henry Hardy and Roger Hausheer, 628–37. London: Chatto and Windus, 1997.

Bordo, Michael D., Claudia Dale Goldin, and Eugene N. White, eds. *The Defining Moment: The Great Depression and the American Economy in the Twentieth Century*. Chicago: University of Chicago Press, 1998.

Borgwardt, Elizabeth. *A New Deal for the World: America's Vision for Human Rights*. Cambridge, MA: Belknap Press of Harvard University Press, 2005.

Brinkley, Alan. *The End of Reform: New Deal Liberalism in Recession and War*. New York: Vintage, 1995.

——— . *Voices of Protest: Huey Long, Father Coughlin, and the Great Depression*. New York: Vintage, 1983.

Carter, Susan B., Scott Sigmund Gartner, Michael R. Haines, Alan L. Olmstead, Richard Sutch, and Gavin Wright, eds. *Historical Statistics of the United States, Earliest Times to the Present, Millennial Edition*. New York: Cambridge University Press, 2006.

Chandler, Lester V. *America's Greatest Depression, 1929–1941*. New York: Harper and Row, 1970.

Cohen, Andrew Wender. *American Monetary Policy, 1928–41*. New York: Harper and Row, 1971.

——— . *The Racketeer's Progress: Chicago and the Struggle for the Modern American Economy, 1900–1940*. Cambridge: Cambridge University Press, 2004.

Cohen, Lizabeth. *Making a New Deal: Industrial Workers in Chicago, 1919–1939*. Cambridge: Cambridge University Press, 1990.

Eichengreen, Barry. *Golden Fetters: The Gold Standard and the Great Depression, 1919–1939*. New York: Oxford University Press, 1992.

——— . "The Origins and Nature of the Great Slump Revisited." *Economic History Review* 45, no. 2 (1992): 213–39.

Fearon, Peter. *Origins and Nature of the Great Slump, 1929–1932*. Atlantic Highlands, NJ: Humanities Press, 1979.

——— . *War, Prosperity, and Depression: The U.S. Economy, 1917–1945*. Oxford: Philip Allan, 1987.

Feinstein, Charles H., Peter Temin, and Gianni Toniolo. *The European Economy between the Wars*. New York: Oxford University Press, 1997.

Fraser, Steve, and Gary Gerstle, eds. *The Rise and Fall of the New Deal Order, 1930–1980*. Princeton: Princeton University Press, 1989.

Hawley, Ellis W. *The New Deal and the Problem of Monopoly: A Study in Economic Ambivalence*. Princeton: Princeton University Press, 1966.

Jacobs, Meg. *Pocketbook Politics: Economic Citizenship in Twentieth Century America*. Princeton: Princeton University Press, 2005.

Kennedy, David M. *Freedom from Fear: The American People in Depression and War, 1929–1945*. New York: Oxford University Press, 1999.

Kindleberger, Charles Poor. *The World in Depression 1929–1939*. London: Allen Lane, 1973.

Leuchtenburg, William E. *Franklin D. Roosevelt and the New Deal, 1932–1940*. New York: Harper Torchbooks, 1963.

——— . *The FDR Years: On Roosevelt and His Legacy*. New York: Columbia University Press, 1995.

——— . *The Perils of Prosperity, 1914–1932*. Chicago: University of Chicago Press, 1993.

——— . *The Supreme Court Reborn: The Constitutional Revolution in the Age of Roosevelt*. New York: Oxford University Press, 1995.

——— . "When the People Spoke, What Did They Say?: The Election of 1936 and the Ackerman Thesis." *Yale Law Journal* 108, no. 8 (1999): 2077–114.

Maher, Neil M. *Nature's New Deal: The Civilian Conservation Corps and the Roots of the American Environmental Movement*. New York: Oxford University Press, 2007.

Olson, James S. *Saving Capitalism: The Reconstruction Finance Corporation and the New Deal, 1933–1940*. Princeton: Princeton University Press, 1988.

Patterson, James T. *America's Struggle against Poverty, 1900–1985*. Cambridge, MA: Harvard University Press, 1986.

——— . *Congressional Conservatism and the New Deal: The Growth of the Conservative Coalition in Congress, 1933–1939*. Westport, CT: Greenwood Press, 1981.

——— . *The New Deal and the States: Federalism in Transition*. Princeton: Princeton University Press, 1969.

Phillips, Sarah T. *This Land, This Nation: Conservation, Rural America, and the New Deal*. New York: Cambridge University Press, 2007.

Romer, Christina D. "The Great Crash and the Onset of the Great Depression." *Quarterly Journal of Economics* 105, no. 3 (1990): 597–62.

——— . "What Ended the Great Depression?" *Journal of Economic History* 52, no. 4 (1992): 757–84.

Rothermund, Dietmar. *The Global Impact of the Great Depression*. London: Routledge, 1996.

Rowley, William D. *M. L. Wilson and the Campaign for the Domestic Allotment*. Lincoln: University of Nebraska Press, 1970.

Saloutos, Theodore. "New Deal Agricultural Policy: An Evaluation." *Journal of American History* 61, no. 2 (1974): 394–416.

Schulman, Bruce J. *From Cotton Belt to Sunbelt: Federal Policy, Economic Development, and the Transformation of the South, 1938–1980*. Durham, NC: Duke University Press, 1994.

Skidelsky, Robert. *John Maynard Keynes: A Biography*. 3 vols. London: Macmillan, 1983–2000.

Smith, Jason Scott. *Building New Deal Liberalism: The Political Economy of Public Works, 1933–1956*. Cambridge: Cambridge University Press, 2006.

Volanto, Keith J. *Texas, Cotton, and the New Deal*. College Station: Texas A&M University Press, 2005.

Weir, David R. "A Century of U.S. Unemployment, 1890–1990: Revised Estimates and Evidence for Stabilization." *Research in Economic History* 14 (1992): 301–46.

Table 1. Major federal acts of the Great Depression and New Deal

Name of action	Citation	Date	Description
Reconstruction Finance Corporation Act	47 Stat. 5	1/23/32	Created Reconstruction Finance Corporation (RFC), capitalized at $500m and permitted to issue obligations worth up to three times as much, to aid banks and other industries.
Glass-Steagall Act	47 Stat. 56	2/27/32	Permitted Federal Reserve System to issue notes backed by government securities.
Federal Home Loan Bank Act	47 Stat. 725	7/22/32	Created Home Loan Bank System, patterned on Federal Reserve System, to permit rediscounting of mortgage loans.
Emergency Banking Relief Act	48 Stat. 1	3/9/33	Title I recognized a banking emergency, empowered the president to halt bank transactions and the secretary of the treasury to impound gold. Title II empowered the comptroller of the currency to appoint conservators for banks, investigate their books, and determine their soundness. Title III authorized the RFC to buy and sell bank stock. Title IV liberalized the Federal Reserve System's authority to issue advances to member banks.
Civilian Conservation Corp Reforestation Relief Act	48 Stat. 22	3/31/33	Authorized the president to create a "conservation corps among the unemployed," which became the Civilian Conservation Corps (CCC), chiefly for the maintenance of public lands.
Agricultural Adjustment Act	48 Stat. 31	5/12/33	Title I recognized a state of agricultural emergency and disparity between rural and urban incomes which it would be

(Continued)

Table 1 (*Continued*)

Name of action	Citation	Date	Description
			policy to redress; directed the secretary of agriculture to create Agricultural Adjustment Administration (AAA) to regulate production of commodities and administer processing tax. Title II, or the Emergency Farm Mortgage Act, expanded federal power to back farm mortgages. Title III, or the Thomas Amendment, authorized the president to issue paper money and determine the gold or silver weight of the dollar.
Federal Emergency Relief Act	48 Stat. 55	5/12/33	Declared an economic emergency of unemployment and failure of local relief funds, allotted $500m of RFC money for a Federal Emergency Relief Administration (FERA) to grant as relief to the states.
Tennessee Valley Authority Act	48 Stat. 58	5/18/33	Created the Tennessee Valley Authority (TVA) to maintain and operate Wilson Dam and Muscle Shoals and to improve navigation and control floods in the region, extending to transmission of electrical power and manufacture of fertilizer and explosives.
Securities Act of 1933	48 Stat. 74	5/27/33	Required corporations to register securities with the Federal Trade Commission to prevent fraudulent issues.
Home Owners' Loan Act	48 Stat. 128	6/13/33	Created the Home Owners' Loan Corporation (HOLC) to refinance mortgages on residences and prevent foreclosures.
Banking Act of 1933 (Glass-Steagall)	48 Stat. 162	6/16/33	Increased power of the Federal Reserve Board to oversee transactions of Federal Reserve System, created the temporary

Banking Act)			Federal Deposit Insurance Corporation (FDIC), limited commercial banks' ability to trade in securities.
National Industrial Recovery Act	6/16/33	48 Stat. 195	Title I recognized a state of industrial emergency, suspended anti-trust law, and authorized the president to create an agency to address the emergency by the composition of industrial codes; Roosevelt created the National Recovery Administration (NRA). Title II authorized the president to create a Federal Emergency Administration of Public Works, which became the Public Works Administration (PWA), to lend and grant $3.3bn appropriated for this purpose.
Civil Works Administration	11/9/33	Executive Order no. 6420B	Roosevelt created the Civil Works Administration (CWA), funded with $400m from the National Industrial Recovery Act, "for the purpose of increasing employment quickly."
Gold Reserve Act	1/30/34	48 Stat. 337	Placed control of monetary gold in the federal government and authorized the president to establish the gold value of the dollar for a two-year period at not more than 60 percent of its current value; established a stabilization fund in the Treasury.
Securities Exchange Act	6/6/34	48 Stat. 881	Created Securities and Exchange Commission (SEC) and empowered it to regulate trading of securities on the stock exchange.
National Housing Act	6/27/34	48 Stat. 1246	Created the Federal Housing Administration (FHA), funded out of the RFC, to insure mortgages.

(Continued)

Table 1 (*Continued*)

Name of action	Citation	Date	Description
Joint Resolution for Enforcement of National Industrial Recovery Act	48 Stat. 1183	6/19/34	Authorized the president to create a board to enforce section 7a (collective bargaining) of the National Industrial Recovery Act. Roosevelt created the National Labor Relations Board (NLRB).
Emergency Relief Appropriation Act of 1935	49 Stat. 115	4/8/35	Appropriated $4.9bn for emergency relief use.
Resettlement Administration	Executive Order no. 7027	4/30/35	Under the Emergency Relief Appropriation Act of 1935, Roosevelt created the Resettlement Administration (RA) to aid the migration of poor farm families. In 1937 RA became the Farm Security Administration (FSA) within the Department of Agriculture.
Works Progress Administration	Executive Order no. 7034	5/6/35	Under the Emergency Relief Appropriation Act of 1935, Roosevelt created a system for evaluating proposed projects including the Works Progress Administration (WPA), "to move from the relief rolls to work ... the maximum number of people in the shortest time possible."
Rural Electrification Administration	Executive Order no. 7037	5/11/35	Roosevelt created Rural Electrification Administration (REA) to support the extension of electrical power using funds from the Emergency Relief Appropriation Act of 1935.

National Labor Relations Act (Wagner Act)	49 Stat. 449	7/5/35	Created new NLRB to replace the board created by executive order in 1934, to assure specified rights of employees to organize and bargain collectively and prevent defined unfair labor practices.
Social Security Act	49 Stat. 620	8/14/35	Title I provided for grants to states for old-age assistance. Title II provided for federal old-age benefits. Title III provided for grants to states to administer unemployment compensation plans. Title IV provided grants to states for aid to dependent children. Title V provided grants to states for maternal and child welfare. Title VI allotted money to states for maintaining public health services. Title VII established a Social Security Board to study and recommend "the most effective methods of providing economic security through social insurance." Titles VIII and IX levied taxes on employers and employees to support the program. Title X provided grants to states for aid to the blind.
Banking Act of 1935	49 Stat. 684	8/23/35	Title I made the FDIC permanent. Title II amended the Federal Reserve Act to establish the Board of Governors of the Federal Reserve System, appointed by the president, and lodged powers to regulate the supply of money, establish credit policy, and supervise banks with them.
Public Utilities Holding Company Act	49 Stat. 803	8/26/35	Defined a public interest in public utilites, enumerated abuses of that public interest, and made it policy to eliminate such abuses and also to eliminate holding companies.

(Continued)

141

Table 1 (*Continued*)

Name of action	Citation	Date	Description
Soil Conservation and Domestic Allotment Act	49 Stat. 1148	2/20/36	Aimed at achieving agricultural parity through conservation measures.
National Housing Act Amendments of 1938	52 Stat. 8	2/3/38	Amended National Housing Act to make it easier to resell mortgages. RFC created National Mortgage Association of Washington, later renamed the Federal National Mortgage Association (Fannie Mae), to resell mortgages.
Agricultural Adjustment Act of 1938	52 Stat. 31	2/16/38	Established the yardstick of normal wheat yields and paid farmers to meet this target.
Fair Labor Standards Act	52 Stat. 1060	6/25/38	Established national minimum wage and maximum hours, banned child labor.

Index

Index

Expand your collection of
VERY SHORT INTRODUCTIONS